Leading Every Day

124 Actions for Effective Leadership

SECOND EDITION

A JOINT PUBLICATION

JOYCE KASER   SUSAN MUNDRY

KATHERINE E. STILES   SUSAN LOUCKS-HORSLEY

CORWIN PRESS
A SAGE Publications Company
Thousand Oaks, California

This book is a product of WestEd's National Academy for Science and Mathematics Education Leadership. The Academy was supported by the National Science Foundation under Contract #9619007. Any opinions, findings, and conclusions or recommendations expressed in this publication are those of the authors and do not necessarily reflect the view of the National Science Foundation.

For information:

Corwin Press
A Sage Publications Company
2455 Teller Road
Thousand Oaks, California 91320
www.corwinpress.com

Sage Publications Ltd.
1 Oliver's Yard
55 City Road
London EC1Y 1SP
United Kingdom

Sage Publications India Pvt. Ltd.
B-42, Panchsheel Enclave
Post Box 4109
New Delhi 110 017 India

Printed in the United States of America.

Library of Congress Cataloging-in-Publication Data

Leading every day:124 actions for effective leadership / Joyce Kaser . . . [et al.].— 2nd ed.
    p. cm.
"A joint publication with National Staff Development Council (NSDC) and Corwin Press"—Publisher.
Includes bibliographical references and index.
ISBN 978-1-4129-1640-0 (cloth) — ISBN 978-1-4129-1641-7 (pbk.)
    1. Educational leadership—Handbooks, manuals, etc. 2. School management and organization—Handbooks, manuals, etc. I. Kaser, Joyce S.
LB2805.L345 2006
917.91'32-dc22   2005018974

This book is printed on acid-free paper.

09   10   9   8   7   6   5   4

Acquisitions Editor:	Elizabeth Brenkus
Editorial Assistant:	Candice L. Ling
Production Editor:	Diane S. Foster
Copy Editor:	Pam Suwinsky
Typesetter:	C&M Digitals (P) Ltd.
Proofreader:	Chloe Kristy
Indexer:	Molly Hall
Cover Designer:	Michael Dubowe
Graphic Designer:	Scott Van Atta

◈ Contents

Susan Loucks-Horsley

1947–2000

This book is dedicated to our coauthor and dear friend, Susan Loucks-Horsley, whose visionary leadership and tireless dedication to education reform inspired so many. The National Academy for Science and Mathematics Education Leadership (on which this book is based) was a dream realized for Susan. For many years, she had talked with colleagues about the need to build the next generation of leaders for education. She had a vision of a leadership academy that would be a national network, in which leaders learned from and supported each other. The academy she developed and directed, like Susan's many other endeavors, was a tremendous success. Through this and other achievements, she carried out the work she cared so passionately about—the continual improvement of education for children and professional development opportunities for educators.

Susan will live on in the work and hearts of the many people with whom she shared herself so generously during her remarkable career. We give tribute to her and promise to carry on her vision and passion for leadership development. Susan's middle name was Hope, and she had it in abundance. Our hope is that her work lives on in you as you take up and use the ideas and reflections on leadership, change, learning, and group facilitation in this book.

—Joyce S. Kaser, Susan Mundry, and Katherine E. Stiles

⬛ Acknowledgments

Translating the curriculum of the National Academy for Science and Mathematics Education Leadership into the 124 contemplations in this book was not a solitary task. First and foremost, we are grateful to those who contributed to the first edition, including our WestEd colleague Kathy DiRanna, whose spirit and enthusiasm for the Leadership Academy and for this book has continued to energize us. Our special thanks go to the Leadership Academy fellows, mentors, learning colleagues, and advisors who reviewed the first edition and offered valuable suggestions and insights. For this we thank Richard Audet, Susan Brady, Karen Falkenberg, Kelly Jacobs, Page Keeley, Nancy Kellogg, Paul Kuerbis, Emma Walton, and Sybil Yastrow. We thank Kendall Zoller who, in addition to his review of the manuscript, wrote material for Book Four. Friends and colleagues of the authors who provided input and background information for the first edition include Stan Altrock, Terry Brill, Nancy Love, Marilyn Lutz, Norm Mitchell, Judith Noel, Ronald Richmond, Marlene Ross, and Robert Terry. Thanks also go to Diane Enright, who helped us finish a quality first edition manuscript.

The second edition of *Leading Every Day* would not have been possible without the continuous lessons learned we have gleaned from our Leadership Academy colleagues. They have taught us so much about leadership development, sharing with us the ways in which they use the first edition of this book with their peers, supervisors, colleagues, and clients. We are especially grateful to Page Keeley and Cheryl Rose, Nelson Letts, Stacey Roddy, and Emma Walton for their suggestions on how to engage various learners with the content of the book.

Our special thanks goes to Deanna Maier of the Leadership Academy staff, who prepared the final manuscript and made numerous helpful suggestions. We appreciate her hard work and dedication.

Our colleagues at Corwin Press provided the motivation and guidance in producing both the first and second editions, and we gratefully thank Robb Clouse and Elizabeth Brenkus for always finding a niche for our ideas, and Pam Suwinsky for helping us refine our words.

We also want to gratefully acknowledge the National Science Foundation. Their confidence in Susan Loucks-Horsley's vision and support for the Leadership Academy enabled us to reach hundreds of science and mathematics education leaders.

Finally, we thank our families, who—yet again—have allowed us the space and time to write while providing unconditional support throughout the process of preparing the manuscript.

The contributions of the following reviewers are gratefully acknowledged:

Kevin Fitzgerald, Principal
Caesar Rodney High School
Camden, DE

Stephen Handley, Principal
Terry High School
Terry, MS

Page Keeley, Senior Science Program Director
Maine Mathematics & Science Alliance
Augusta, ME

Randall Lindsey, Principal Associate of the Robbins Group
Director, Education Leadership Doctorate Program
California Lutheran University
Thousand Oaks, CA

Emily Moore, Professor
Educational Leadership & Policy Studies
College of Education
Iowa State University
Ames, IA

Jenny Mudgett, Principal
Caldwell Elementary School
Auburndale, FL

Ann Porter, 2002 NAESP National Distinguished Principal
Lewis & Clark Elementary School
Grand Forks, ND

Dennis Sparks, Executive Director
National Staff Development Council
Oxford, OH

▧ About the Authors

Joyce S. Kaser (EdD, American University, Washington, D.C.), is a Senior Program Associate with WestEd. She is also President of Kaser and Associates and a Senior Research Associate with The Study Group. She is first author of *Enhancing Program Quality in Science and Mathematics*, also published by Corwin Press. This book presents an approach, called *profiling*, to formative evaluation of programs that support mathematics and science education. Over the past 15 years, she has been one of the key developers of this methodology. She has also been an evaluator of a number of large-scale change efforts across the country, along with numerous national and statewide professional development programs. She is the author of a *Guide to Identifying and Selecting Quality Professional Development in Mathematics and Science*, a tool for school and district personnel that is found on the Web sites of four key organizations. Currently, she is part of a team developing the framework for a National Assessment of Educational Progress science assessment to be administered nationally in 2009. A former teacher and school administrator, she is coauthor of a change management methodology for use in education, along with a risk analysis assessment process for large system interventions. This second edition reflects her most recent work in professional development, evaluation, change management, lifelong learning, and group leadership.

Susan Mundry is Associate Director of Mathematics, Science, and Technology Programs at WestEd. She also codirects the National Academy for Science and Mathematics Education Leadership, which prepares educators to lead educational improvement efforts in science and mathematics. Susan was also Senior Research Associate for the National Institute for Science Education's professional development study and dissemination team. She coauthored several books and educational materials, including *Designing Effective Professional Development for Teachers of Science and Mathematics* (Corwin Press, 2003); *Global Perspectives for Local Action: Using TIMSS to Improve U.S. Mathematics and Science*

Education (National Academy Press, 1999); *Leading Every Day* (Corwin Press, 2002); and *Teachers as Learners* (Corwin Press, 2003), a set of videotapes, a guidebook, and Web site activities that illustrate diverse strategies for teacher learning in science and mathematics. She is codeveloper of *Leading and Learning,* a simulation game on leadership development. In 2002, Susan served as the chair for the National Science Teachers Association Task Force on Professional Development. Prior to joining WestEd, Susan served in many roles from staff developer to Associate Director at The NETWORK, Inc., a research and development organization focused on organizational change and dissemination of promising educational practice. There she led several technical assistance projects and oversaw the work of the National Center for Improving Science Education and the Center for Effective Communication. Susan was a contributor to many studies and projects for these Centers and developed the "Change Games"—two widely used simulations on educational change, entitled *Making Change for School Improvement* and *Systems Thinking/Systems Changing.*

 **Katherine E. Stiles** is a Project Director and Senior Research Associate at WestEd. She is codirector of WestEd's National Academy for Science and Mathematics Education Leadership. Katherine was the Principal Investigator of a National Science Foundation (NSF)-funded Research, Evaluation, and Technical Assistance (RETA) grant—the Academy for Professional Development in Science and Mathematics—which was designed to support the Math and Science Partnership (MSP) initiatives. The RETA builds on and extends the work in professional development reflected in *Designing Professional Development for Teachers of Science and Mathematics,* (Corwin Press, 2003) of which Katherine is a coauthor of both the first and second editions. She is a senior staff member on TERC's Using Data Project and conducts professional development for data teams and provides technical assistance to participating schools in Ohio and Arizona as they engage in this three-year project to enhance science and mathematics student achievement through collaborative inquiry into data. Katherine has more than 10 years of experience evaluating science education and professional development programs, including NSF-funded Local Systemic Change projects and State Systemic Initiatives, California-funded MSP projects, technology-based science education programs, and science curriculum development projects. Prior to joining WestEd in 1995, Katherine worked at the National Science Resources Center in Washington, D.C., as a science curriculum developer and authored four curriculum units for the *Science and Technology for Children* program. With degrees in psychology, special education, and education, and teaching experience in elementary programs, she brings 20 years of experience to her current work in science and mathematics education and professional development.

Susan Loucks-Horsley was Associate Executive Director at Biological Sciences Curriculum Study (BSCS) and Senior Research Associate for Science and Mathematics at WestEd. She directed the Professional Development Project at the National Institute for Science Education and was senior author of the project's *Designing Professional Development for Teachers of Science and Mathematics*, published in 1998. Previously, she was the Director of Professional Development and Outreach at the National Research Council (NRC) Center for Science, Mathematics, and Engineering Education. Her work at the NRC included promoting, supporting, and monitoring the progress of standards-based education, especially the *National Science Education Standards*. Her work as Associate Director of the Northeast/Islands Regional Lab and the National Center for Improving Science Education focused on developing approaches, products, and training activities to help educators build their knowledge and skills in collaborative approaches to staff development, program change, and program evaluation. She led the development team of *Facilitating Systemic Change in Science and Mathematics Education: A Toolkit for Professional Developers*, a product of the 10 regional education laboratories. She was senior author of *Continuing to Learn: A Guidebook for Teacher Development, An Action Guide for School Improvement, Elementary School Science for the '90s*, reports from the National Center for Improving Science Education on teacher development and support, and numerous chapters and articles on related topics. While at the University of Texas (Austin) Research and Development Center for Teacher Education, she worked on the development team of the Concerns-Based Adoption Model (CBAM), which describes how individuals experience change.

About the National Academy for Science and Mathematics Education Leadership

S ince 1997, the Leadership Academy has supported leaders throughout the United States—from Puerto Rico to Alaska—to implement wide-scale science and mathematics education reform through in-depth professional development experiences. The Leadership Academy's curriculum focuses on leadership styles, practice, and models; organizational and individual change; strategic planning and organizational development; facilitation and development of collaborative groups; data-driven decision making; and professional development design, implementation, and evaluation.

The first three cohorts of leaders were supported with funding from the National Science Foundation; and cohorts four, five, and six have been supported with funding from the Susan Loucks-Horsley Educational Fund and individual tuition. During the past 8 years, participating leaders have achieved many impressive outcomes. They have put some of the best resources for learning in place, returned to their own settings to lead learning for others, contributed to the knowledge base by writing and publishing books, developed new approaches to teacher professional development, advanced their careers, and most important, improved outcomes for teachers and students.

The Leadership Academy is a project of WestEd—a research, development, and service agency working with education and other communities to promote excellence, achieve equity, and improve learning for children, youth, and adults. It was started in collaboration with several national organizations:

- Association for the Education of Teachers in Science (AETS)
- Association for State Supervisors of Mathematics (ASSM)

- Council of State Science Supervisors (CSSS)

- National Council of Supervisors of Mathematics (NCSM)

- National Staff Development Council (NSDC)

- National Science Education Leadership Association (NSELA)

- National Science Teachers Association (NSTA)

- National Research Council's Center for Science, Mathematics, and Engineering Education (CSMEE)

For additional information about the Leadership Academy, contact WestEd's Tucson Office: 622 North Country Club Road, Suite "E," Tucson, AZ 85716. Telephone: (520) 888–2838. Fax: (520) 888–2621.

▧ Introduction

Welcome to the second edition of *Leading Every Day: 124 Actions for Effective Leadership.* If you have read the first edition, a special "Welcome back" to you. We were delighted with the impact of the first edition and with the many people who shared their stories of how the book influenced their practice. The book was recognized by the National Staff Development Council with the 2003 Outstanding Book of the Year Award. This new edition has been substantially updated. Our underlying purpose—helping you to be an effective leader during a time of rapid change—remains the same. However, informed by new research and thinking in the field, our suggestions for getting you there have been reshaped and sharpened.

Most of the content in this book is part of the curriculum of the National Academy for Science and Mathematics Education Leadership, which provides participants with the knowledge and perspectives to carry out their roles as leaders. The primary audience for this book is leaders—leaders at all levels of the system. We consider leaders to be anyone who facilitates the learning and work of and with others, including teacher leaders, principals, district administrators, state-level coordinators, and those from higher education, technical assistance agencies, and informal learning institutions.

Leading Every Day is divided into four books: Leadership Every Day, Leading Change, Leading Learning Communities, and Leading Effective Groups. These four topics are, in the authors' experience, the key areas for developing and sustaining leaders. For each book, the material is presented in 31 contemplations, one for each day of the month. Each contemplation begins with an inspiring quote, discusses important aspects of the topic, and ends with a reflection, usually a series of questions or a scenario for the reader to consider.

So, what's different about the second edition? Book One, Leadership Every Day, and Book Three, Leading Learning Communities, have been completely revised. Over the past 4 years we have continued to work closely with leaders who have shaped our experiences and learning; thus, our own learning has led us to make some shifts. In addition, Book Three has been completely revised to reflect the new content in the second edition of *Designing Professional Development for Teachers of Science and Mathematics* (Corwin Press, 2003).

The focus of Book Two, Leading Change, and Book Four, Leading Effective Groups, has been sharpened. Book Four focuses on the work of Bob

Garmstom and Bruce Wellman, and we gratefully thank the authors and their publisher, Christopher-Gordon, for allowing us to include so much of their work in *Leading Every Day.*

During the past 4 years, there has been a wealth of new research and literature about how people learn, the relationship of leadership practices to improved student learning, the role of data to guide improvement efforts, and the value of developing schools as professional learning communities. This new research has guided our revisions in this edition of the book.

For example, there's more discussion in this edition about the ethics of leadership, especially being a moral leader. We know more about how people develop expertise and transfer learning from one context to another, and these ideas are reflected in several contemplations throughout the book. There's a greater emphasis on the use of data for decision making, leading change, and designing adult learning experiences based on student needs. In response to reader's requests, there are new contemplations on how leaders can take care of themselves by preventing burnout in themselves as well as others. The four books are more closely integrated, with several themes interwoven throughout the entire volume. The references, bibliographies, and examples have been updated in each book.

The contemplations of *Leading Every Day* can be read in order, or a reader may select a specific theme to pursue throughout the four books. However you choose to engage with this volume, the contemplations are best read in an environment that is conducive to reflection, when you have time and energy to consider the questions and compose thoughtful and meaningful responses.

The revisions noted enhance readers' individual and personal exploration into developing their leadership knowledge and skills. Another addition to our revisions is the *Facilitator's Guide for Leading Every Day* (Corwin, 2005). The guide, published simultaneously with the second edition of this book, provides suggestions on how to use *Leading Every Day* with groups of people. Creating the facilitator's guide was in direct response to readers' requests for additional resources to help them use *Leading Every Day* with others.

In the spirit of continuous learning, we hope that the contemplations in *Leading Every Day* and the accompanying *Facilitator's Guide* help readers reflect on their leadership roles, styles, and practices. We believe that the insights leaders gain will sustain them through challenging transitions.

Book One

◈ Leadership Every Day

At no other time in education have we needed quality leadership more than we do today. Schools are striving to support all students to meet challenging standards. This requires rethinking how schools operate, developing new roles for teachers and administrators, and changing expectations as well as behaviors.

Without supportive and proactive leadership, the increased pressure for high performance can be exhausting and demoralizing. It can encourage blaming and lead people to lose hope. With visionary and moral leadership, schools and the people in them feel supported as they focus on improving processes and practices and work together to achieve high performance. They can set a course for success, monitoring and celebrating milestones, and supporting one another along the way.

Quality leadership is a team sport. It requires collaboration among many to make it work well and practice, practice, practice to get it right. With today's challenges and opportunities in education we need many, rather than a few, people leading collaboratively and creatively every day.

The contemplations in Book One introduce leadership as a way of thinking and acting every day. They are organized by major themes, including:

- What do effective leaders do? How do they build a shared commitment to the work? What specific practices increase student achievement?

- What are the environments that support excellent leadership, such as shared leadership and professional learning communities?

- What are some of the challenges leaders face, and how can they address them?

- What are the traits of leaders, and how do they keep doing the right things?

These topics are interwoven through the contemplations for Days 1 through 31.

DAY 1

We Are All Leaders

A community is like a ship; everyone ought to be prepared to take the helm.

—Henrik Ibsen

Are you a leader?

Have you wrestled with this question maybe once or twice in your life, or maybe more frequently? Do you eagerly take responsibility for leading others, or is it harder for you to take the helm? What does it mean to you to be a leader?

One common definition of *leadership* is an individual's ability to work with others to accomplish some agreed-upon result. What *isn't* in this definition is as important as what *is*. It says absolutely nothing about position, title, or status.

Everyone can demonstrate extraordinary leadership when he or she learns and uses effective practices such as those described in this book. You do not need to be an administrator to be a leader. Sometimes having an impressive job title helps to get things done, but not always. In fact, when leaders rely only on their positional power to make things happen, their coworkers or followers may be *compelled* to do what the leader wants, but they may not be *committed* to their work. The ability to use personal power positively to influence others and build commitment to the goals and the work is a hallmark of a good leader.

In a study on leadership in education reform sites, Murphy and Datnow (2002) identified that principals, teacher leaders, and others all play key roles in supporting school improvement. Effective principals are catalysts for change, protectors of the vision, and leaders of inquiry, engaging others in exploring questions versus telling everyone what to think. They are willing to let go of leadership functions associated with their roles and support shared leadership among all staff.

◈ Reflection

The greater your ability to influence and mobilize others, the greater your capacity for leadership, no matter what your position is in the organization.

Consider how prepared you are to be an effective leader. Do you:

- Have a clear vision of what you want and how you can contribute?

- Trust and empower others to take on leadership responsibilities and roles?

- Rely on positional power less than your ability to engage with and influence others?

- Actively seek ways to develop leadership in others?

- What are your strengths? What would you like to enhance?

◈ Notes

DAY 2

What Do Effective Leaders Do?

When the best leader's work is done the people say, "We did it ourselves."

—Lao-tsu

According to an extensive database compiled by Kouzes and Posner (2002), leaders who accomplish extraordinary results with others use five leadership practices. Their actions contribute to their effectiveness and the success of those with whom they work. Effective leaders use these five leadership practices:

1. *Model the way.* It is no surprise that effective leaders are credible. People usually know what to expect from them. They are clear about their own personal values and views and build a consensus among others about the values that will guide all of them. Leaders "model the way" by checking to make sure their actions are consistent with their values, sending a strong message about what is important to them and their work.

2. *Inspire a shared vision.* Effective leaders care deeply about what they want to accomplish and work with their colleagues to identify common, shared goals and aspirations for the future.

3. *Challenge the process.* Effective leaders question and work to change the status quo. They take on challenging projects that help them learn something new. They learn from their failures as well as their successes and think about every day as a chance to do their job smarter and better than the day before.

4. *Enable others to act.* Leaders foster collaboration and teamwork. They share power and responsibility. They actively remove hierarchy and other roadblocks to increase interactions among people who need to work together. They coach and support others so that they have the confidence they need to succeed. They continually ask themselves, "What can I do to help this person continue to grow and be highly competent?"

5. *Encourage the heart.* Effective leaders build a strong caring community in which people praise and recognize success. They know success breeds success and celebrate each small milestone. They support and encourage everyone when the going gets tough. (Kouzes & Posner, 2002)

Effective leaders intentionally and deliberately use these practices every day.

◈ Reflection

How often do you demonstrate the leadership practices described? Review the short descriptions of each, and rank order them from those you do most frequently to those you do least frequently. Reflect on the ones you practice frequently. How well are you performing these practices? What would you like to do better?

Reflect on the ones you practice infrequently. How might you use these more often? What support do you need to do that? Who can help you?

Here are some examples of behaviors related to the leadership practices. How might you incorporate these into your daily practice?

- For a week, make a list of every task you perform. About each ask yourself, "Why am I doing this? Why am I doing it this way? Can this task be eliminated or done better?"

- Establish a norm of asking everyone to share things they have done recently to enhance performance and outcomes.

- Ask staff to identify areas in the organization that need improvement. Commit to changing three of the most frequently mentioned items.

- Write down what you aspire to accomplish in your current position and why. Talk with others about their hopes and goals. Find areas of common goals and shared aspirations that you can work on together.

- Publicize the work of your colleagues. Let others know about their accomplishments.

- Think about what you say and do each day for a week. Are your actions consistent with your values? If you say you believe in creating a place where all students will succeed, are your behaviors supporting that vision? Are you setting the example you want? If there are inconsistencies, identify what you need to change. (Kouzes & Posner, 2002)

◈ Notes

_____

_____

_____

_____

_____

DAY 3

Making Conscious Choices

One's philosophy is not best expressed in words; it is expressed in the choices one makes.

—Eleanor Roosevelt

Choose. Choose often—hundreds of times a day, in fact.

Choose. Choose based on what you desire—what you truly want for yourself and others.

Choose. Choose deliberately and consciously. Choose, if you want to move forward. Don't choose, and you stay stationary or fall back.

One of the key characteristics of leaders is that they consciously make all kinds of choices—not just the big ones, such as instituting new policies or restructuring schools. They make medium-sized choices, such as choosing not to blame themselves for failure or not being deterred from their mission by adversaries. They also make many small choices: choosing to check in on a colleague who has a serious illness in the family or picking up the coffee cups at the end of a meeting. And each of the choices leaders make says something about what they stand for and what they want for themselves and their organizations.

As a leader in your organization, there are two choices that are essential for you to make:

1. *Choose to know what you want.* Oftentimes, people cannot move ahead because they don't know what they want. They are stagnant, often waiting for some external force to push them in a direction. Although it is not easy, you can develop a conscious habit of knowing what you want and pursing it. Maybe you need to set up a meeting with an influential person in your community to help get the budget passed; perhaps you want to get small groups of staff working together to better track the results you are having; or maybe you would rather not serve on a group or committee that you have been assigned to for years. Be clear about and consciously choose what you want. Think of yourself as always having an answer to the question, if it were posed, "What is it that you want right now? Five days from now? Five years from now?"

2. *Choose to act to achieve what you want.* How much of your time do you spend doing what you want to do to achieve your goals? How often do you feel

as if you are compelled to spend time doing things that are not connected to your goals but imposed on you? Listen to your language as you talk with others. How often do you say you "have to" or "should" do something?

According to Dave Ellis (2002), this language communicates that you are living in a world of obligation—your actions are controlled by external influence, not by your own goals and desires. Ellis points out that people communicate more powerfully when they clarify what they want and speak less in terms of what they "have to" do and more in terms of what they "plan" or "promise" to do. People often don't get what they want because they never make their wishes known to themselves and others and act on them. The sheer act of stating what you want will accomplish a great deal. Perhaps to achieve what you want, you must take a next step: set a meeting date, write a memo, or recommend a new program. Each day, try to take at least one step that moves you toward your goals.

◈ Reflection

During the day, stop periodically to ask yourself what choices you are making and why. If you want something at that moment, what is it? Take an extra minute or two for yourself if you don't readily have an answer to that question. Chances are that you do want something—maybe even just 5 minutes to call home or to sign a contract for your next professional development activity. Once you find what it is, choose it for yourself. At the end of the day, tally what you gained for yourself and your organization by making conscious, deliberate choices.

Look over your list. How many of the items relate directly to what you are trying to accomplish? How can you do more of these things and less of the things that may not affect your goals?

◈ Notes

_____

_____

_____

_____

_____

DAY 4
Moral Leadership

Moral purpose means acting with the intention of making a positive difference in the lives of employees, customers, and society as a whole.

—Michael Fullan

Are you a moral leader? Do you act out of a relentless commitment to improve the quality of something or someone? Do you carefully consider what is the right thing to do? Do you have a moral purpose—wanting to make a difference where it matters most?

Leaders must have the highest standards and ethical strength. Their character is always on display—followers ask, "Did she do what she said she would do?" "Do his actions reflect what is valued in our culture and conform to the highest professional principles?" They are quick to point out when leadership behavior is inappropriate, self-serving, and misaligned with the values of the organization.

Moral leaders stand for something—and use every opportunity to communicate their stand to others. One of the leaders from our Leadership Academy dedicated himself to ensuring that all students—especially those from the poorest backgrounds—would have a quality mathematics and science education. He supported a team of terrific leaders to make changes in what and how students were taught and has been rewarded with impressive results. Their students are gaining acceptance to college at record rates and meeting challenging state standards. Leaders like this are willing to stand up and say it is unacceptable for only some students to achieve and to find a way to make things better. They don't quit when it gets tough—when they hit a roadblock, they find another way. Having such a commitment and building relationships with others who share that commitment serves as armor and protection from the ethical dilemmas leaders face.

▦ Reflection

Do you have a strong commitment to making a difference? What is your moral purpose?

Ask yourself, "Have I done everything I can in the best possible way to reach this purpose? What else needs to be done? How am I modeling for and engaging with others to build a community committed to moral purpose and leadership?"

◈ Notes

DAY 5

Using Power Appropriately

When the power of love overcomes the love of power, the world will know peace.

—Jimi Hendrix

What do you think of when you hear the word *power* being used in relation to people, as in "She's a powerful woman" or "He's got a lot of power in this organization"?

Power can be defined as having great influence and control over others. Leaders gain it through positional authority and/or by earning respect and developing a following. Regardless of how leaders gain power, they must use it appropriately and morally. If they fall in love with the idea of power, they may end up taking actions that are in the interest of retaining their power, not in meeting their mission.

Stephen Covey (1990) identified three different types of power used by leaders. When a leader uses *coercive* power, followers follow because they are afraid. They will either be punished in some way or lose something if they fail to do what the leader wants. For example, too often we see education leaders use accountability for student learning as a threat instead of as an opportunity to work together to solve problems. When a leader relies on *utility* power, followers follow because of the benefits they will receive if they comply. This model sees the leader-follower relationship as transactional—the follower will do something for some reward (for example, paycheck, bonus, or recognition). This type of power is the most commonly used in organizations. The third type—*legitimate* power—is focused on building commitment and trust. Followers follow because they believe in the leaders, trust them, and want to achieve the same purpose. This is the type of power that is the strongest and most effective.

Each type of power has different consequences. Coercive power relies on fear and works only as long as there is something to be feared. Although it is based on equity, utility power often encourages individualism rather than group efforts. Legitimate power relies on mutual respect and honor and produces a sustained, proactive response from followers.

◈ Reflection

Pay attention to your own language. Do you often cite the consequences of noncompliance, as in "Those who fail to do this will . . ."? If so, you may be drawing too heavily on coercive power. Do you make promises, as in "Those who do this will get extra credit, a raise, a bonus. . ."? If so, you may be overrelying on utility power. Pay attention to the times you may use these words and think about whether it would be more effective to build trust and commitment so that people are more personally motivated to make desired changes.

After considering these questions, ask yourself what type of power base you see yourself relying on most frequently. How do followers respond? What type of power base would you prefer to use more often? How do you think followers would respond?

◈ Notes

_____

_____

_____

_____

_____

_____

_____

_____

DAY 6
Building Shared Vision

Few, if any, forces in human affairs are as powerful as shared vision.

—Peter Senge

Vision! What is your reaction to this word?

Is it negative? Perhaps you have been involved in vision-building activities that never really made a difference in how your organization functioned or in your results. Perhaps your organization, like many others, failed to live by its vision once it was created.

Effective leaders engage people throughout the organization in building commitment toward the shared vision that becomes the guiding force for all action. A great example of this is schools that have established a vision of an unyielding commitment to ensuring that all students meet local standards. The vision drives all behaviors and informs all of the school's operations, structures, and allocation of resources. Another example is schools that envision themselves as providing the best quality instruction, without exception. Again, the vision shapes what the staff does, including making sure every teacher is supported to learn and carry out best practice and use ongoing analysis of data and results to find out what is working and what needs to be changed.

Many organizations have vision and mission statements. Most visions, however, are not shared visions. They are imposed on others by the head of the organization or a group of people at the top. These visions are not effective long term because they "command compliance—not commitment" (Senge, 1990, p. 206). A shared vision is different. A shared vision incorporates individual visions, engenders commitment, and focuses energy. As Senge (1990) says, "When people truly share a vision, they are connected, bound together by a common aspiration. Shared visions derive their power from a common caring" (p. 206).

Kouzes and Posner (2002) suggest that leaders inspire people to come to a shared vision that is appropriate for them based on carefully considering how future trends will affect them and what reputable people are predicting about their business in the next 10 years. As leaders you must look at this information and identify patterns to predict how you will be affected in the future and help to build a shared vision based on that. Schools that have visions based on old trends and data from prior decades are going to be locked in the past.

Don't confuse vision and mission. *Vision* is knowing where you want to be or what you want to become. It includes tangibles, as well as intangibles, such as virtues and the culture that you want to surround you. *Mission* is your reason for being and the work you pursue to realize your vision. Your mission guides your actions to achieve what you envision for yourself and your organization. Both are necessary, especially for leaders of organizations.

◈ Reflection

Do the people in your organization have a common, clear, and shared vision of what you are working toward? How well does the vision drive decisions and actions? Does it permeate your organization's culture and decision making on a daily basis? Do you have a personal vision for yourself? Are you clear about your mission in life?

◈ Notes

_____

_____

_____

_____

_____

_____

_____

_____

DAY 7
Leading With Diversity

If we are to achieve a richer culture, rich in contrasting values, we must recognize the whole gamut of human potentialities and so weave a less arbitrary social fabric, one in which each diverse human gift will find a fitting place.

—Margaret Mead

Consider the following scenario: You meet a new staff member at the fall orientation. You quickly discover that this person graduated from your alma mater, has relatives in your hometown, lives two blocks away from you, and has children the same age as yours. Such similarities often facilitate a quick and immediate bond. The two of you agree to have lunch soon to get better acquainted.

Here is a different take: You meet a new staff member who was born in Peru. This person speaks fluent Spanish, is single with no children, has traveled extensively around the world, is a technology expert, and keeps two exotic birds as pets. You don't speak Spanish, are married with several children, haven't traveled outside the United States, are technology anxious, and are philosophically opposed to keeping exotic animals or birds as pets. You think that you have little in common with this person. Are you more likely to set up a lunch or walk away and meet someone else? If you are like most other human beings, you will move on to someone else. However, think for a moment how much you might learn from this person.

While it is much less challenging to be with others of one's own culture, ethnicity, socioeconomic group, or religion, interactions among people with varied backgrounds can offer the greatest learning opportunities. Leaders have a responsibility to model the value of diversity and create opportunities for everyone to associate with a variety of people, share perspectives, and promote deeper understanding.

Leaders can promote diversity through formal team-building activities as well as informal groupings and assignments. Mix people up in learning situations and in team assignments. Set up opportunities for everyone to share their backgrounds, cultures, and what they consider as the strengths they bring to creating a diverse perspective in the organization. During staff or team meetings, ask people to speak from a particular diverse perspective. For example, have wide representation of different groups provide input to a decision you are making. Ask staff to point out when an action or a decision may not be in the best interest of all groups. Find alternatives that better serve everyone.

▧ Reflection

How do you ensure diversity in your organization? Whom do you involve to ensure a broad perspective? How are work groups of various kinds structured? When people are free to choose, with whom do they choose to work?

What is the turnover rate in your organization? Does it differ based on race, ethnicity, gender, or other similar factors?

What is the racial, ethnic, and gender composition of your administrators and organizational leaders? How do they model the importance of seeking diverse involvement and building unity among all?

What more can you do to demonstrate the value of diversity?

▧ Notes

_____

_____

_____

_____

_____

_____

_____

_____

DAY 8

Leading for Results

If I have seen farther than others, it is because I was standing on the shoulders of giants.

—Isaac Newton

Current leaders can learn so much from the leaders that have come before us. We all benefit from knowing what has worked for other leaders and getting insight into the question, "If you can only use a few leadership practices, what is likely to have the greatest results?" For example, what leaders do in schools can have a significant impact (positive or negative) on student learning. In a meta-analysis of 30 years of research on leadership, Waters, Marzano, and McNulty (2002) identified 21 leadership practices that enhance student achievement. They are many of the actions we discuss throughout the volume for leaders to use in general. Savvy school leaders actively seek to use these practices:

1. Building culture by fostering shared beliefs and a sense of community and cooperation

2. Maintaining order by establishing a set of operating procedures and routines

3. Protecting teachers from distractions that will take away from their teaching time or focus

4. Providing resources such as professional development and materials to support staff to do their jobs

5. Directly involving themselves in the design and implementation of curriculum, instruction, and assessment practices

6. Establishing clear goals and keeping the focus on meeting them

7. Being knowledgeable about curriculum, instruction, and assessment practices

8. Having quality interactions with staff and students and being visible

9. Recognizing and rewarding individual accomplishments

10. Communicating effectively with staff and students

11. Reaching out to stakeholders and being a strong advocate for the school

12. Seeking input and involving staff in decisions and policy making

13. Recognizing school accomplishments and acknowledging failures

14. Building strong relationships with staff

15. Being change agents willing to challenge the status quo

16. Providing leadership and inspiration for new and challenging innovations

17. Taking action based on strong ideals and beliefs about education

18. Monitoring and evaluating effects on student learning

19. Adapting leadership style to the situation and being tolerant of dissent

20. Knowing the school context and using your understanding of people and situations in your context to solve problems

21. Ensuring that staff have opportunities for intellectual stimulation around the work of teaching and learning

◈ Reflection

These are the effective leadership actions shown to best influence student learning. To what extent have you developed the capacity to use them? For those of you who are or who work with principals and school leaders, what are some ways you can increase the use of these practices that are tied to student achievement?

What gets in the way of using these research-based practices in schools? Review the list and select three you think could have a significant impact on your own leadership. What are they? What will you need to do to learn to use them? What is your plan for making them a part of your leadership repertoire?

◈ Notes

_____

_____

_____

_____

_____

DAY 9

Taking Data-Based Action

An individual without information cannot take responsibility; an individual who is given information cannot help but take responsibility.

—Jan Carlzon

What is one piece of information that changed your life?

Can you think of a circumstance in which you read a book, participated in a professional development experience, analyzed student data, or discussed a problem with a friend—and you came away with a completely new perspective that led you to take an action you wouldn't have taken otherwise?

Information is changing life in schools. Staff are using the tools and developing the habits of mind to analyze their data and results, and this practice alone is opening up possibilities for leadership at all levels. By disaggregating student results by gender, race, ethnicity, and poverty level, staff are beginning to focus attention on the areas in need of improvement and to confront whether and how the school works for all students.

Faculty are using data on their results to set goals, implement new practices, and enhance outcomes. Through collaborative dialogue about their results they are able to focus more on what needs to be done and engage in conversations that are grounded in facts and research versus opinions. They are clearer about the outcomes they desire for staff and students and know how well they are doing in terms of reaching the outcomes.

As a leader, what you think, say, and do has a profound affect on the quality of the collaboration, the culture of the school, and student learning. In one of our projects, school teams use a collaborative inquiry process to move away from the practice of sharing information with only a few people to building learning communities with many change agents making widespread use of data (Love, 2002). Effective leaders build these collaborative structures to support staff to work together and use data to see where they are in relation to meeting goals for student learning. They share information widely, so that all staff have the opportunity to gain insights into how well they are meeting their goals, areas for improvement, and areas for celebration.

◈ Reflection

It is critical for all staff to know what they are working toward and have good information on how they are progressing toward their goals. Here are some questions to ask yourself about the information available in your setting:

- Does your organization value the use of data and information to drive improvements? How do you know?

- Do the staff have the information and data necessary to examine results and make continuous improvements?

- Are data used or abused? Do people use data to find fault and "blame" people, or are they using data to ask how they can improve their systems and processes without blame?

- What can you do personally to increase the exchange of information and the use of data to drive decisions and enhance practice?

◈ Notes

_____

_____

_____

_____

_____

_____

_____

_____

_____

DAY 10

Generating and Sharing Knowledge

Knowledge can't be separated from the communities that create it, use it, and transform it. In all types of knowledge work, people require conversation, experimentation, and shared experiences. . . .

—Etienne Wenger

One of the critical skills for leaders is the generating and sharing of knowledge. Leaders need to "create new settings conducive to learning and sharing that learning" (Fullan, 2001, p. 79).

Nowhere is that organizational value emerging more clearly than in education. Information about best practices, networks, and research on teaching and learning abound in today's publications. Part of a leader's job is to help staff get access to and apply information so that it becomes actively used in practice.

So, as a leader, you need to establish an environment for bringing new knowledge to your staff and encourage them to share information and knowledge with each other. Here are some of the ways we see people in our Leadership Academy build knowledge in their teams:

- *Generating knowledge from practice:* Teams try out new teaching and learning strategies, and share artifacts and examples of how they worked. They document what they learned. One of our participants worked with a colleague on a commercially published book that documents the use of science journals. She spread her knowledge from her own colleagues to teachers nationwide. In another project we are involved with, teachers are generating knowledge of students' misconceptions by using common assessments and comparing their student responses to the research on misconceptions. Educators also produce knowledge by conducting discrete action research projects, discovering what works, and sharing that knowledge with colleagues.

- *Reading and applying research results:* Other teams read and discuss journal articles related to issues or problems they face. They discuss, "To what extent are the findings or issues illuminated in the research generalizable to our situation? How might we apply the research findings?"

- *Learning strategies and approaches from others:* Educators are organizing study groups in which staff read and discuss cases, books, and other information to inform their own thinking and practice.

These organizational arrangements that bring staff together to share and create knowledge are "de-privatizing" education and contributing to increased collegial cultures.

◈ Reflection

Think of a meeting that you will be attending in the next couple of weeks. Is it an opportunity to share and/or generate knowledge that will inform practice in your organization? How might you design the meeting to be knowledge sharing and/or producing? Sometimes all it takes is setting aside time in the meeting for one person to bring work they are doing, share it with others, and allot time for thinking about how others might use or adapt it. Often it involves group members identifying and trying outside resources and learning how they work. Sharing this information and getting in the practice of managing your knowledge is a hallmark of effective organizations.

Assume you have as part of your job description the generation and sharing of knowledge. Make a list of the specific ways that you might carry out that function through your leadership. Who else needs to be involved? Consider how you can develop a norm of having everyone document learning and asking one person to share what they are learning at each meeting or through other communication with staff.

◈ Notes

_____

_____

_____

_____

_____

_____

DAY 11

Keeping a Client-Centered Focus

Consumers know more about what they want—and are more determined to get what they want—than ever before.

—Jim Taylor

Think about a time you felt that you didn't get the service you wanted, needed, and deserved. Perhaps you had taken time off to have someone come fix an appliance, and that person didn't show up and didn't call. Maybe you had paid a bill, but the accounting department kept sending you statements. Possibly you had made arrangements with your supervisor to take a personal leave day, but he or she had forgotten and scheduled you into a meeting.

Try to remember what you were feeling. Frustration? Anger? Resentment? Now, think of just the opposite situation.

Think about a time you were treated as a valued customer. Perhaps the accounting department notified you of an overpayment. Maybe someone from your clinic called to tell you that the doctor was running late. Possibly your supervisor stopped by to make sure that you had everything you needed to get the proposal in on time.

More and more leaders are finding it essential to adopt a client-centered focus. Take education as an example. The ultimate customers are the students and the community. In the old paradigm, if students did not have basic skills in reading and mathematics, it was their fault. After all, they had the opportunity to learn, didn't they? If that situation occurs now, schools are more inclined to look at their own systems to determine what else can be done to ensure that the students reach the learning goals. Their core mission is to teach students, not just to "deliver" lessons.

Students, their parents, and the community are external customers, but there are also internal customers—the colleagues with whom you work. It is important to maintain a client-centered focus with them also. Having a client-centered focus means always thinking about how you can provide great service and making sure that people receive value.

❧ Reflection

Here are a few key questions to ask yourself to gauge your "client centeredness."

- Who are your primary clients or customers—both internal and external?

- What do your customers value? How do you know?

- Are you providing them with what they value?

- What improvements are needed?

- How do you continuously assess your clients' satisfaction?

◈ Notes

_____

_____

_____

_____

_____

_____

_____

_____

_____

DAY 12
Recognizing and Celebrating Success

In the end people will forget what you said, forget what you did, but people will never forget how you make them feel.

—Maya Angelou

In the Day 2 contemplation of this book we introduce five practices used by ordinary leaders to accomplish extraordinary results (Kouzes & Posner, 2002). One of the practices—"Encourage the heart"—often surprises people when we teach these practices in our Leadership Academy. Too often as leaders we focus on the "hard" practices of planning, visioning, and the provision of resources and forget the power and energy that comes from making people feel valued and recognized for their accomplishments.

About 15 years ago one of the authors received a note of congratulations from her then-boss. She had just led a team through a very challenging proposal submission that resulted in winning a large contract. In the note, her boss said, "Today we celebrate your work and the great team that came together to produce this project—with you, I would attempt anything." His note conveyed such a deep sense of trust and confidence in what the team had accomplished that it fueled them to take on challenging work and achieve more success. Saying "Thank you" and "Job well done" may be the easiest thing leaders can add to their repertoire. In staff meetings, give the entire team an opportunity to share recent successes. Post letters or notes of praise from clients or coworkers. Kouzes and Posner suggest that leaders should write three thank-you notes a day!

In one organization we worked in, we instituted a peer award that was named after a staff member who exemplified the practice of recognizing and celebrating staff contributions. Each staff member was entitled to give two of these awards per year to their colleagues (individuals or teams) for contributions and successes. The organization funded gift certificates that accompanied the awards. Staff proudly displayed these awards, and they were announced in the organization's weekly newsletter. Using these everyday leadership practices communicates that people are valued and helps to maintain the high morale needed to get challenging work done.

In education, practices such as setting data-driven goals for improvement are helping everyone see what the desired outcomes are, and by publicly sharing data and results, everyone can be clearer about when it's time for celebration! Reward hard work and results, and it will reward you—success breeds success.

◈ Reflection

How often do you recognize, reward, thank, and/or celebrate success in your organization? Are you careful to make sure that everyone who contributes is recognized? Do you have regular systems for peers to recognize each other? Are the goals clear so that everyone knows when you have achieved success? What one or two things can you do to increase recognition and celebration of success?

◈ Notes

_____

_____

_____

_____

_____

_____

_____

_____

_____

DAY 13

Networking

I have seen that in any great undertaking it is not enough for a man to depend simply upon himself.

—Lone Man (Isna-la-wica), Teton Sioux

What networks are you part of, and what types of relationships do you have within these networks? How can you bring these relationships to bear on issues you care about?

There is a natural human desire to work in groups and to work well together. Information of all kinds is both generated and shared through networks of all types: organizational, professional, community, religious, and family. "Working the networks" is one way that leaders exert influence, communicate vision, share information, provide support, enhance continuity, and bring about change.

One of the consistent findings from our Leadership Academy is the value educational leaders derive from networking and learning from each other. They share common problems and strategies they have used. They listen to each other and share perspectives that enrich their abilities to lead in their own contexts. Change in organizations is so complex that it cannot occur without strong relationships among people making up a variety of networks, some that exist within the boundaries of an organization and some that go outside.

Lewin and Regine (2000) point out that people and relationships—how people interact with each other and the nature of the relationships they form—determine the course of change in an organization. They stress that leadership that focuses on people and relationships is a prerequisite for achieving long-term goals.

▩ Reflection

Which relationships provide you with diverse information and help you in your role as a leader of reform? Do you have relationships from different worlds that keep your mind open to new ideas and approaches and keep you from becoming too insular? What new relationships do you need to forge, and what networks do you need to become part of to broaden your influence?

◈ Notes

DAY 14
Reframing Perspective

Too often [leaders and managers] bring too few ideas to the challenges that they face. They live in psychic prisons because they cannot look at old problems in a new light and attack old challenges with different and more powerful tools—they cannot reframe.

—Lee G. Bolman and Terrence E. Deal

One of the greatest skills a leader can bring to a group is the ability to reframe—simply because it is such a difficult task. Through the act of *reframing*—deliberately looking at something through an entirely different lens—we can change our perceptions or our expectations. Any change in one will automatically produce a change in the other.

We get so caught up in our own issues that we may not stop to think that reframing is possible. Actually, reframing may give us solutions we have never even thought of. For example, how hard is it for you to replace "old data" with "new data"?

Think of a time when you wanted to think or feel differently about a person or situation. Even though you tried very hard, altering your frame of reference was very difficult, perhaps impossible.

There is good reason for that. Our frame of reference has two components: our expectations and our perceptions, which are integrally connected. As Daryl Conner (1998) points out, "We expect to get more of what we already see, and we usually can only see that which we already expect. That is why it is so difficult to move away from a perspective once it's established" (p. 317).

In changing our perceptions, we change the way we look at a situation. For example, if you have been making changes in instructional practice, but have failed to raise achievement, you can either call it a failure and forget it or ask yourself, "What can we learn from this?" When you reframe it as an opportunity to learn what is and is not working, you can build on your successes and learn from mistakes to enhance outcomes in the future. If we can't change how we view the situation, we can always change our expectations. For example, if you expect the support of your supervisor in your reform effort and that support is not forthcoming, you will continue to experience frustration. An alternative is to accept the fact that support is not forthcoming and change your strategy.

Thus, in reframing, you purposefully look at the issue from a different angle or develop expectations that are more apt to resolve a situation.

❧ Reflection

Here are some ways to begin reframing:

• Ask yourself what assumptions or beliefs you are applying to the situation (for example, "I am looking at this from the point of view of . . .").

• Is this the best perspective through which to view this situation? Is there another lens that provides a greater opportunity for taking positive action?

• Expand your repertoire of lenses. Ask yourself how someone else would see this—a scientist? A child? A public official? A parent? A CEO of a major corporation?

Try reframing some issue that you are currently dealing with. Be conscious of whether you are altering your perceptions or expectations or both. What is the result?

❧ Notes

_____

_____

_____

_____

_____

_____

_____

DAY 15

Taking Genuine Action

To become a credible leader, first you have to comprehend fully the values, beliefs, and assumptions that drive you. You have to freely and honestly choose the principles you will use to guide your actions.

—James M. Kouzes and Barry Z. Posner

How many times have you done something in a particular way because someone else has done it that way or because someone told you to do it that way?

In reflecting back on her early days, a former teacher told the following story:

> It was a day I'll never forget and an important lesson learned. I was a first-year teacher, only slightly older than my students. In the study hall I was in charge of, there was a young man who would not stop disrupting others through his talking. I recalled another teacher relating how in his classroom he taped students' mouths when they wouldn't be quiet. In my increasing frustration, I grabbed a roll of tape and approached this young man. All of a sudden, I realized that he was bigger than I was, and that did make a difference. Also, I saw this technique as incongruous with what I believed about how to treat students. In my moment of need, I lost my own grounding and grabbed someone else's approach.

We often act without considering whether our behavior is congruent with our own underlying beliefs about what is right. When people assume new leadership roles, existing leaders are often ready to offer advice—for example, one group might tell you to "Be strong, make sure you don't back down. People will be testing you at first, and you will have to be tough." Another might say, "Don't come on too strong right away—you need to get to know everyone and understand what is going on, before you start making changes." What is most important is that you take genuine action that is aligned with what you believe.

Here is a chance for you to determine your basic assumptions about leadership: Do you believe that (a) leaders are born or (b) leaders are made? That (a) leadership is positional (that is, based on their positions, only certain people in organizations are leaders) or (b) everyone in an organization can exert leadership? That (a) leadership exists independently of ethics (for example, Hitler was a leader) or (b) leadership is inherently ethical (for example, Hitler was not a leader)?

Does your behavior indicate that you believe that certain people are blessed at birth with leadership abilities? Or do you act as if everyone can learn to exhibit some degree of leadership if they choose to? Do you see that leadership is vested in people with certain titles, or do you believe in the leadership capacity within all people in an organization? In your belief system, what is the relationship between leadership and ethics? You should be able to tie your behavior to one of the assumptions in each pair. Is your behavior congruent with what you believe, or have you fallen into a pattern of acting inconsistently with what you believe?

What are your beliefs about who can learn? If you are in a school or working with schools, do you believe all students can learn? How genuine are your actions with respect to this belief? For example, while most educators will say all students can learn, the schools are not always organized to ensure that all children learn. Rick DuFour and others (2004) identified four types of schools with different beliefs about who can learn. The "Charles Darwin School" believes students can learn based on their ability. The teachers in these schools see aptitude as relatively fixed and do not believe they can have a great influence on the extent of student learning and they teach accordingly. The "Pontius Pilate School" operates on the belief that all students can learn *if* they take advantage of the opportunity the school provides and put forth the necessary effort. The "Chicago Cubs Fan School" is based on the belief that all students can learn *something* and helps students experience academic growth in a warm and nurturing environment. Only the "Henry Higgins School" operates on the belief that all students can achieve high standards of learning as long as they receive enough support and help from the staff (DuFour, DuFour, Eaker, & Karhanek, 2004, pp. 30–31). Leaders must examine the actions that are taken in the organization and ask, "What beliefs and assumptions are operating in our system that makes us act this way?" Most often people are not even aware of the disconnect between their behaviors and their espoused beliefs.

◈ Reflection

What are the beliefs operating in your organization? If you are in a school or working with schools, which of the four types described most closely matches the beliefs about learning in your setting? What are the beliefs about who can be a leader? What are your assumptions about who can and cannot learn? How do these beliefs influence your actions? How might you surface and discuss the beliefs that may be limiting you?

◈ Notes

DAY 16
Developing Your Culture

Any organization that sets out to change its own culture remains powerfully influenced by that culture even as it attempts the change.

—Robert Evans

What is the culture of your organization?

Daryl Conner (1993) defines *culture* as "the beliefs, behaviors, and assumptions of an organization [that] serve as a guide to what are considered appropriate or inappropriate actions" for individuals and groups to engage in (p. 164). Culture operates at two levels: (1) overtly, as apparent in policies and procedures and (2) covertly, reflected in "the way things are done."

Culture in an organization usually evolves over time. The personalities of the leaders often determine the beliefs, behaviors, and assumptions that eventually become firmly established, although they may not be especially visible. This results in what Conner (1993) calls a *default* culture.

It is much less common for leaders to consciously and deliberately establish the type of organizational culture that serves their needs. As a result, new leaders often inherit a culture that doesn't support changes they want to make in the organization. And they find out quickly that a nonsupportive culture can be very inhospitable to a change initiative.

If you are a leader of a new organization or project, you have the opportunity to build the type of culture you believe works best. If you take over an existing entity, you have the harder task of assessing and changing the culture—a difficult but not impossible task.

Regardless of which position you are in, here are some things to consider about your culture:

- Are the values and principles explicit so that everyone understands what is valued?

- What is the trust level in the organization? Do people at different levels trust one another? What do you do to make it safe for people to take risks and trust one another?

- Are people valued as individuals, or are they thought of primarily as assets or resources?

- Are people's hands, heads, and hearts wanted—or just their hands?

- Is the atmosphere informal and comfortable, or is it formal and tense?

- Are people treated equitably, or is there evidence of preferential treatment?

- Is the environment positive, with people encouraged and recognized, or is it negative, with little or no recognition and a lot of blaming?

- Does the organization freely share information, or is the flow of information tightly controlled?

- Is learning from mistakes valued, or are people more likely to be fired, blamed, or reprimanded for errors or failure?

- Is learning valued, or is it seen as a deterrent to getting the work done?

- Is the organization committed to continuous improvement, or does it change only when there is a major problem? (Gibb, n.d.)

◈ Reflection

Considering this list, to what extent do you have the culture you want? Which areas need further development and work?

Are you in a position to help establish or change the culture? If so, what would be your top three priorities?

◈ Notes

_____

_____

_____

_____

_____

_____

DAY 17

Building a Professional Learning Community

If schools want to enhance their organizational capacity to boost student learning, they should work on building a professional community that is characterized by shared purpose, collaborative activity, and collective responsibility among staff.

—Fred Newmann and Gary Wehlage

Take a good look at your organizational structures and systems. How well do they support the people in the organization to achieve their vision and mission? Most leaders in education inherited organizational structures and systems that were based on the old "factory model" and are completely out of alignment with contemporary goals for education. They tend to focus on establishing efficient procedures and following rules over ensuring results. Decisions are usually centralized, and there is little interest in innovation. Staff are expected to follow procedures, avoid making waves, and are held accountable for teaching (coverage) rather than learning (results). These structures produce a lack of individual responsibility for achieving outcomes and disempower staff.

As leaders work to transform their organizations, they must create new structures that are in greater alignment with current expectations for students as well as the organizational visions and goals, build opportunities for meaningful collaboration, and keep a laser focus on student outcomes and other results.

DuFour and Eaker (1998) assert that to meet the demands and expectations of education today, schools must reorganize themselves as *professional learning communities* (PLCs).

PLCs have these six characteristics:

1. *Shared mission, vision, and values:* The organization is guided by a set of principles that describe what people believe and what they hope to create. The principles are reflected in the actions and beliefs of all the people throughout the school. There is a shared commitment to enacting the principles every day.

2. *Collective inquiry:* PLCs are involved in an ongoing and collaborative quest for ways to increase their effectiveness and deepen their understanding

of their beliefs and actions. Staff engage in a collective inquiry process (Ross, Smith, & Roberts, 1994) that involves public reflection about assumptions and beliefs, coming to shared meaning, engaging in joint planning, and taking action to continuously get better at what they do.

3. *Collaborative teams:* PLCs establish collaborative teams that share a common purpose. They work together regularly to achieve their purpose.

4. *Action orientation and experimentation:* PLCs are organized to take action. They reflect on what is needed, try something, learn from its results and then take action again.

5. *Continuous improvement:* PLCs are always searching for better ways to achieve their results. They continually experiment to find better ways to meet their mission and goals.

6. *Results orientation:* The PLC holds itself accountable for results. The staff identify clear and measurable goals and a data system for tracking them.

Leaders who wish to create professional learning communities in their organizations need to think carefully about how to start. This is a large undertaking, and some leaders choose to start with small teams that learn to examine data, engage in dialogue, and take actions to enhance student learning. The small group might then reach out to involve more and more of the faculty. Other leaders begin by creating opportunities for dialogue among all faculty about the purpose of the school and how well its current structure supports its purpose and move from there. As you consider how to apply these ideas in your own setting, work with all staff to provide a clear vision of what operating as a PLC involves, and invite dialogue about why the approach will or will not work for your organization.

◈ Reflection

To what extent is your organization operating as a professional learning community? Are people living a shared purpose guided by shared beliefs, or are staff members more driven by procedures and rules? Is everyone clear about the desired outcomes and the plan for reaching them? How collectively and collaboratively are people working?

What are the advantages (or disadvantages) you see for your own organization to work in this structure? What additional information would you like to have on PLCs?

◈ Notes

_____

_____

_____

_____

_____

_____

_____

_____

_____

_____

_____

_____

DAY 18

Shared Leadership

School leadership needs to be a broad concept that is separated from person, role, and a discrete set of individual behaviors. It needs to be embedded in the school community as a whole. Such broadening of the concept of leadership suggests shared responsibility for a shared purpose of community.

—Linda Lambert

Traditionally, those at the top of organizations set the policies and procedures, and those at lower levels carry them out. If we are to have many, rather than a few individuals, who are leaders, we must see the value and importance of developing leadership skills and responsibilities at all levels of an organization.

Peter Senge and others advocate for an organizational value called *localness* (Senge, Kleiner, Roberts, Ross, & Smith, 1994). According to this value, "A higher level should not make decisions for a lower level, if the lower level is capable of making the decision itself" (p. 309). This value builds responsibility from the bottom to the top of the organization. Decisions are made by those with the expertise who are closest to the situation. Increasingly, organizations are sharing and distributing leadership to those people closest to the action. In education this means empowering teachers to make the choices of what and how to teach their students guided by data and standards. There is also a growing appreciation for the role teacher leaders play in developing and supporting other teachers, since the teacher leaders have had the experience themselves and are still closely connected to the classroom.

Localness unleashes "people's commitment by giving them the freedom to act, to try out their own ideas and be responsible for producing results" (Senge, 1990, pp. 287–288). Staff are often much more knowledgeable about day-to-day operations and are in the best position to make decisions.

In traditional hierarchical structures in education, administrators tell teachers what programs to implement with little input from the teachers themselves. In schools that value localness and share decision making, teachers have the responsibility and power to ask what would work better and to help choose programs that will solve their unique problems. Leaders need to look for opportunities to challenge and empower people at all levels to solve the problems closest to them.

The value of localness must be balanced with attention to serving the good of the whole. Senge (1990) discusses a phenomenon referred to as "the tragedy of the commons." This occurs when local decision makers, drawing on shared resources, focus only on their needs to the exclusion of the whole; they look at the closest part rather than the more distant whole. This is often a concern voiced by central leaders who do not want to decentralize any control. An example of the tragedy of the commons is the commercial orchard that diverts water for irrigation to fill an immediate need without considering how the action affects farmers farther down the river. In another example, a middle school team selects a new mathematics textbook without considering how it fits into the scope and sequence of the entire K–12 curriculum.

To build a culture of shared leadership while guarding against decisions that do not serve the good of the whole, someone who can influence local decision makers in the organization needs to be involved in making "commons" decisions. This is necessary because it is sometimes difficult for those at the local level to see the broader implications of their actions.

◈ Reflection

How is leadership shared in your organization? Are the people who are closest to the problem or process responsible for everyday decisions and for helping to support and coach those close to them to do the best job? Are the people empowered to lead at all levels clear about their responsibilities and their authority?

What decisions are best made at the level at which you are working? Which ones should be made at a lower level? At a higher level? Are you vulnerable to any "tragedy of the commons" misperceptions? How can you guard against these?

◈ Notes

DAY 19

Solving Problems

A problem well stated is a problem half solved.

—John Dewey

Think back to a recent problem you were trying to solve. Do you recall how you went about it? There are four important factors to look at in problem solving. Leaving out one or more will usually produce a decision that won't stand the test of time. Here is what should be included (Myers, McCaulley, Quenk, & Hammer, 1998):

1. *Examine the facts.* What do you know about the problem? Dig deeply— what is really happening?

2. *Consider the possibilities.* Consider possible causes of the problem and alternative solutions. Use the most imaginative thinking available.

3. *Evaluate the situation logically.* Perhaps this involves making a list of the pros and cons of any possible solution or analyzing cause-and-effect relationships (that is, if you do x, then y is likely to happen).

4. *Look at the impact of your proposed solution on people, including yourself and your own value set.* How will your solution affect other people? Yourself? Is it congruent with your value system? Is this what you really want for your-self and your organization?

Here is an example of the importance of these factors in making decisions: A director of a professional association fired a relatively new employee who had falsified 15 minutes on her time sheet. He took this one fact, that she had misrepresented 15 minutes, and used it as the basis for letting her go. At no time did he consider any extenuating circumstances that might have led to her falsifying her time. Neither did he consider the impact of his decision on his staff, who marched into his office demanding to know what had happened. This young woman had performed well so far and had started to develop relationships with others within the organization.

As the story unfolded, the director discovered that the woman had not known how to record her brief absence and had done so incorrectly. There was no malicious intent on her part. The director called her to apologize and to ask her to return. It was too late; she was angry at the way she had been treated and had already found another job. In this case, he had relied on looking at a fact and evaluating it logically, ignoring other possibilities and the impact on people. Had he considered these two other factors, he would likely have made a different decision, or at least gathered more information before taking action.

◈ Reflection

Just like the man in the story, most of us rely on two of these four factors in addressing problems and making decisions, often to the exclusion of the other two. Which two are your favorites? Which two are you most likely to ignore or skip over?

Think of a problem you are facing. Work through a solution the way you normally do. Now, take into account all four factors, following the guidelines listed. Is the resolution different? If so, how?

◈ Notes

_____

_____

_____

_____

_____

_____

_____

DAY 20
Building Relationships

Relationships are all there is. Everything in the universe only exists because it is in relationship to everything else. Nothing exists in isolation. We have to stop pretending we are individuals who can go it alone.

—Margaret Wheatley

If Wheatley (2002) says that relationships are all there is, and Fullan (2001) says that "you can't get anywhere without them," relationships and their cultivation are crucial to successful people, friendships, colleagueships, and organizations.

Whether in organizations or in families or among friends, relationship problems often determine the future and fate of an institution, a marriage, or a friendship. Productive relationships are critical for organizations and the people who make up these organizations to survive.

Think for a moment of the problems you are currently facing. How many involve a relationship problem with a colleague, a friend, or member of your family? Can you pinpoint the underlying cause?

Within the last few years, the emotional intelligence (EQ) work of Goleman (1995), Goleman, Boyatzis, and McKee (2002), and Stein and Book (2000) has expanded our knowledge of the importance of strong relationships in human and organizational functioning, the skills essential for forming and maintaining effective relationships, and how to diagnose and heal relationship problems. So what are the components of emotional intelligence? Stein and Book name five realms:

1. *Intrapersonal:* Self-awareness, actualization, independence, and self-regard

2. *Interpersonal:* Empathy, social responsibility

3. *Adaptability:* Problem solving, flexibility

4. *Stress management:* Stress tolerance, impulse control

5. *General mood:* Happiness, optimism

A high level of skill in these five areas is essential for relationship building and maintenance. As Fullan says, "If relationships are (almost) everything, a high EQ is a must" (p. 74). Your leadership ability—that is, your ability to influence others—is directly related to your relationship EQ.

⬥ Reflection

Look at the five components of emotional intelligence listed. How do you assess yourself on each? Put an *S* next to those that are strengths and a *W* next to those you see as weaknesses. If you are currently experiencing relationship problems, are any of the weaker elements contributing to them? What can you do to strengthen at least one area of weakness (for example, increase your tolerance of stress or become more flexible in your thinking)?

⬥ Notes

_____

_____

_____

_____

_____

_____

_____

_____

_____

DAY 21
Trying Something New

The only true insanity is doing the same thing over and over and expecting different results.

—Rita Mae Brown

Think of a time you felt stymied by your attempts to change a frustrating or irritating situation. Have you found yourself doing the same thing over and over? Or perhaps the same thing with only slight variations? How readily do you change what you are doing to better meet others' needs?

In such situations, we often think that the problem is with the other person, people, or organization. However, we cannot control the behavior of anyone but ourselves. With that as a given, here are two different approaches for breaking the cycle:

1. *Reframe the situation.* You can turn a perplexing problem into a marvelous opportunity for learning by reframing. It is possible to transform what appears to be a failure into a test case, which failed in some ways, succeeded in others, and yielded great learning. The entry for Day 14 outlines such a reframing process.

2. *Change your behavior.* There are always myriad things you can do. Use a different approach. Treat the person differently. Be kinder or firmer. Give more help or less help. Talk more or talk less. Be more independent or ask for help. If you are not sure what behavior to change, ask for advice from a trusted colleague.

Either reframing the situation or changing your behavior increases your chance of seeing some behavior change on the part of the other person. It is likely to work better than continuing to do whatever you have been doing that has not been getting the desired results.

◈ Reflection

Think of a time you repeated the same behavior but expected different results. Were you eventually able to break out of the pattern? If so, what happened? How do you recognize when you are caught in a cycle? Which of the techniques described is most useful in helping you respond differently?

◈ Notes

_____

_____

_____

_____

_____

_____

_____

_____

_____

_____

_____

_____

DAY 22

Coping With Ambiguity, Change, and Confusion

Entering the era of perpetual unrest means confusion, mixed feelings, and ambiguity are here to stay.

—Daryl Conner

Have you ever found yourself thinking that surely life will slow down when the current crisis or demand on your time is over? We often hope that our lives will be more manageable, slower paced, or less hectic when some major event ends. What happens is that when one event is over, another takes its place. And they keep coming, so that we never experience the respite we wish for.

The reality is that the days of small, incremental changes, which we could not only incorporate but often prepare for, are gone. As Daryl Conner (1998) describes, "The world is inundated with disruptions: unforeseen dangers, unanticipated opportunities, unmet expectations, alarming new statistics, startling twists of fate, shocking innovations, unheralded improvements, unrealistic requirements, overwhelming demands, contradictory directives, staggering liabilities, astonishing results, sudden strokes of luck, and more" (p. vi).

What, then, does it take for leaders to cope with continuous ambiguity, continuous change, and continuous confusion? Here are three major strategies:

1. *Accept ambiguity, change, and confusion as the norm rather than the exception.* The degree to which you experience stress is directly related to your expectations. If you expect your life to move slowly in a harmonious fashion, you may be upset when a meeting is canceled at the last minute, your car breaks down, or you leave your computer at the security gate. If you know that you are subject to many external forces and that the only thing you have control over is how you choose to react, you are much better equipped to deal with inevitable ambiguity, change, and confusion. Anchoring yourself in your core values and beliefs will give you additional support in weathering change.

2. *Be resilient.* Your ability to deal with the unknown is much greater if you have a high level of resiliency. Your outlook and attitude are important, as well as how you handle the daily stressors. Do you know how to release anger? Relieve frustration? Handle criticism and failure without internalizing? Do you have a support system to rely on? Do you get away from work on a regular basis and take care of yourself physically and emotionally? These are all ways to be a resilient person, one who is capable of maintaining his or

her productivity and quality standards along with physical and emotional stability while assimilating change (Conner, 1993).

3. *Act anyway.* Unless you are content to be paralyzed by your fear or to attempt escape to a more peaceful place and time, you have no choice other than to move ahead. Move ahead despite the continuous ambiguity, continuous change, and continuous confusion. Use your best available information and move forward with your fear and anxiety in hand, rather than attempting to repress or escape from your feelings. Do each day the best you can.

Another way of saying this is to "put a lion in your heart." "To fight a bull when you are not scared is nothing," says a well-known bullfighter, "and not to fight a bull when you are scared is nothing. But to fight a bull when you are scared—that is something" (von Oech, 1992, p. 51). What gives you the courage to act on your ideas? Having a well-thought-out plan? Encouragement? Faith in the idea? Past success? What puts a lion in your heart?

▧ Reflection

On a scale of 1 (low) to 10 (high), how do you rate your ability to cope with ambiguity and to assimilate change? Which of the three strategies listed do you rely on to cope with major changes? What can you do to strengthen your capacity to deal with a constant state of flux?

▧ Notes

_____

_____

_____

_____

_____

_____

DAY 23

Balancing Leadership and Management

Managers are people who do things right, while leaders are people who do the right thing.

—Warren G. Bennis

What is leadership and what is management?

Both are very important in organizational life and shouldn't be confused.

Leadership is doing the right thing; management is doing things right. Managers direct the hacking of a new path through the jungle; leaders make sure that they are in the right jungle.

One of the major contributions that a leader can make is to always be able to distinguish between these two important functions. We often become so focused on the day-to-day realities of what we do that we lose sight of whether we are doing the right thing.

Leaders often have to ask the hard questions: Are we getting the best results possible? Where can we improve? Who is not learning and what can we do about it? Are there ethical issues involved? What knowledge and skills do our staff need, and how will they get them? Will the proposed staff development give us what we need? Is our strategic planning council effective? These queries will help you challenge the status quo that is often accepted without question.

❧ Reflection

Think about the leadership role you play and ask yourself the following questions:

• Why are you doing what you are doing? What data do you have to show that you are addressing the right problems and doing the right work?

• How are you spending your time? What percentage of your day is spent on managing tasks? What percentage is focused on setting the course, engaging with others and providing leadership?

• Are you sure you are "doing the right things" before you set up procedures to "do things right"?

• What beliefs and assumptions drive your leadership approach? Are these consistent with where you want to be?

▨ Notes

DAY 24

Living With Paradox

The contradictions of life are not accidental. Nor do they result from inept living. They are inherent in human nature and in the circumstances which surround lives.

—Palmer Parker

Inevitably, anyone in a leadership role encounters people and circumstances that reflect inherent contradictions. These are called paradoxes. Paradoxes stem from conflicting polarities: the existence of two opposing attributes, tendencies, or principles that are interdependent. For example, in large organizations, there is often tension between the desire to centralize and the desire to decentralize procedures and services. Having both operational in a system is the paradox. Another example is the need to work in teams versus working individually. Polarities and the paradoxes they create are ever present; they never go away.

Leaders in education encounter many paradoxes that they need to thoughtfully balance as they lead improvement efforts. For example, Bybee (1993) identified this set to describe the paradoxes leaders must balance as they carry out change efforts in their organization.

Leaders must:

- Think abstractly and act concretely

- Have direction and retain flexibility

- Initiate change and maintain continuity

- Encourage innovation and sustain tradition

- Fulfill a national agenda and incorporate local mandates

- Achieve goals and endure criticism (pp. 164–166)

Successful leaders recognize and work through both sides of the paradoxes. The first step in working with them is knowing one's own biases. We tend to prefer one side of the pole over the other. We must see the validity of both sides, recognizing the simultaneous existence of opposites. The second step is to discuss how to address each one. For example, how will you pursue achieving the goals if you are being criticized? What things will you maintain and which will you change?

If your organization is focusing on one side of a polarity as the solution to a problem, your role as a leader is to alert people to the other. For example, if your colleagues are pushing for a concrete set of action steps to address a problem, work on that together and then ask the team to think abstractly about their plan—what values do they think it represents? What will they look for in terms of results? Likewise, as leaders work with their teams to lay out a direction for the organization, they also must ask what might happen that would cause them to change their direction. How can you remain flexible enough to respond to feedback and changes in the environment? Your role as a leader is to balance both sides of the polarity and not allow one side to dominate to the exclusion of the other (Terry, 2001).

◈ Reflection

What paradoxes do you face in your work? Which side of the polarity are you biased toward? What can you do to make sure that the other side of the polarity is considered and addressed?

◈ Notes

_____

_____

_____

_____

_____

_____

_____

DAY 25

Paying Attention to Leadership Actions and Traits

Energetic-enthusiastic-hopeful leaders "cause" greater moral purpose in themselves, bury themselves in change, naturally build relationships and knowledge, and seek coherence to consolidate moral purpose.

—Michael Fullan

In our Leadership Academy we ask participants to recall a time when they were particularly effective as a leader and to bring to mind their actions as well as the personal characteristics or dispositions they exhibited at the time. As they share their stories and experiences, it becomes clear that leadership actions and personal traits work hand in hand to support quality leadership. They report taking actions such as:

- Developing and communicating a clear purpose

- Holding high expectations for everyone

- Anticipating and addressing small problems before they grow into bigger ones

- Demonstrating a deep understanding of the work

- Developing others

- Facilitating change

But as they take these actions, they are also using personal characteristics that contribute to their success, such as being action oriented, enthusiastic, realistic, risk taking, caring, and committed. They underscore the importance of having integrity and being a listener and a learner and willing to change their minds. What emerges from this exercise is a composite of actions and traits of effective leadership. High performance leadership comes from balancing key leadership actions with personal dispositions that strengthen and support leadership results.

Michael Fullan (2001) writes that all of us can become better leaders by focusing on just a few key leadership capacities. He developed a framework for leadership depicting five capacities for leaders to lead complex change. Many of these actions are ones we address with individual reflections in this book, including:

1. Moral purpose

2. Understanding change

3. Building relationships

4. Promoting knowledge creation and sharing

5. Coherence making

Fullan wraps these leadership capacities in three personal characteristics—energy, enthusiasm, and hope—that both build and reinforce the five capacities. For leaders to achieve high performance they need their actions and dispositions to work in harmony.

◈ Reflection

Think about a time you saw someone demonstrate tremendous leadership skill. What did they do that contributed to their success? What personal characteristics did they possess and how did these support their actions?

What personal characteristics do you draw on to enhance and support your own leadership skills? How hopeful and positive are you? Do you avoid expressions of doubt and convey confidence in yourself and your team? How do you display enthusiasm for your work? Can people feel your energy, or are you seen as worn out and exhausted by the demands of your leadership position? How can you reenergize yourself?

◈ Notes

_____

_____

_____

_____

_____

_____

DAY 26
Getting Support

The person who tries to live alone will not succeed as a human being. His heart withers if it does not answer another heart. His mind shrinks away if he hears only the echoes of his own thoughts and finds no other inspiration.

—Pearl S. Buck

In most of the contemplations in this book so far we talk about what actions effective leaders take to support other people and the organization, but there are also things you need to do for yourself to feel supported in your leadership role. To keep up your energy, enthusiasm, and sheer will to get things done, you need ample support from and contact with others and to be able to call on them when you need help and inspiration. Leadership comes with a tremendous amount of stress—for example, sometimes things don't work out the way you had hoped, people are resistant to your ideas, and forces out of your control undo your actions. When these situations occur, leaders may feel like they are out there all alone. As one leader described it, "I feel like I am rolling a tremendous boulder uphill—and if I stop for a moment, it will come tumbling down on me and no one else will be there to help me catch it."

One of the fellows in our Leadership Academy gets the support she needs by talking with other administrators outside of her district who have been in her shoes. She gets their feedback on what she is trying to do in her own district and asks how they would handle a similar situation—she does the same for them. When she goes to conferences or regional events in her state she actively talks with others in her role to ask them what has worked for them—and then she asks them if she can stay in touch via e-mail or phone. She has put together her own personal network. It is not unusual for us to get a call from her that starts with, "Hello, I am calling 911—here's what happened and I need to think it through with you." Usually, she had thought through what she needed to do, but just needed that extra ear and reassurance that she hadn't missed something. At the end of the call she will say, "Thanks, you are a lifesaver!" Having support like that can be a lifesaver, since it relieves the stress and loneliness of leadership that can wear you out.

Good leaders recognize that they do not have to do it all themselves. It is okay to "dial 911" when you need support—it is not a sign of weakness, but rather a sign that you are aware of what you need for yourself to be an effective leader for others. In *Primal Leadership* (2002), Goleman and others suggest that sometimes leaders reach a point of burnout or exhaustion, and they need to have time to refresh and regroup. Sabbaticals, formal opportunities to engage in reflection, and getting a new assignment can help reawaken leaders and set them back on successful paths.

Leaders begin to build networks of support by talking with people who have similar roles in their own organization or geographic area. They actively ask others to share their perspectives on different situations and ask for honest feedback from colleagues. They identify what support they need from supervisors and communicate those needs to them.

◈ Reflection

• What have you done for yourself lately to reduce loneliness and get support?

• When you feel the stresses of being "the leader" closing in on you, how do you take care of yourself? Who do you talk with? What else can you do?

• What do you need from your supervisor to feel more supported? How can you communicate your wishes and get what you need?

• If your organization provides sabbaticals, consider how taking time to work on a sabbatical project could reinvigorate you.

◈ Notes

DAY 27
Asking Good Questions

The important thing is to never stop questioning.

—Albert Einstein

In the Day 2 contemplation in this book, we share five practices effective leaders use to accomplish extraordinary results. One of them—"Challenge the process"—recognizes that leaders today must continuously ask how to get better and improve outcomes. They ask, "Why are we doing what we are doing? Why are we doing it this way? Are there more effective things we can do?" (Kouzes & Posner, 2002).

In today's fast-paced world, leaders can't possibly have all the answers. They need to use good questions to guide others to get to the "right answers." Peter Scholtes (1998) identified "seven basic all-purpose questions" leaders must ask (p. 266):

1. *Why?* When you encounter a problem, ask why. Ask why as many as five times to get to the root cause of the problem.

2. *What is the purpose?* People love to suggest things and often grab onto new ideas to implement in their organizations without making sure there is a match between the organization's needs and their ideas. Help people clarify the purpose—or the desired outcome—as they plan new projects.

3. *What will it take to accomplish this?* While it is nice to dream, your job as a leader is to support people to implement their ideas. This question gets others to think through the methods they will use to put ideas into action.

4. *Who cares about this?* Ask this question to make sure you are choosing actions that will matter to the right people. If the people you serve notice or care about the action, it should have higher payoff for you.

5. *What is your premise?* Many suggestions and ideas are made without stating the assumptions or beliefs that are guiding them. When you ask people to state their premise or assumption, you help them gain greater insight.

6. *What data do you have or could you get?* Some suggestions and ideas are based on perceptions and hunches—asking this question pushes people to "ground" their actions in real data.

7. *What is the source of your data?* Before you base decisions on data, make sure it is valid and comes from a reliable source.

Increasingly, a leader's role is to coach colleagues to think through plans, anticipate problems, and get the right things happening. Questioning and demonstration are the basic tools of a good coach. Here are some other questions that Scholtes suggests leaders ask when a team is implementing a new project or intervention:

Prior to Starting

- What could realistically go wrong?

- How might that be prevented?

- What should we monitor to see if the problem is occurring?

- How can we be prepared to react if it goes wrong? (p. 273)

During Implementation

- What are you doing?

- Why are you doing it?

- How do you know this is the right thing to do? (p. 273)

After Implementation

- Are we getting what we wanted?

- Are we avoiding what we didn't want?

- Do we need to make any adjustments? (p. 273)

◈ Reflection

Are you always ready with the answer, or do you help your staff or colleagues think through solutions by asking good questions? How can asking questions help you become a better leader?

Learn to use inquiry and questioning skills as a key part of your leadership style. Choose one of your major goals—for example, maybe it is a goal you have set to enhance student performance. For one week, as you interact with your colleagues, ask them how what they are doing or deciding will influence that one goal. You will see how asking good questions can change the discussion and focus everyone on the key goals.

Copy the seven questions and keep them on your desk or someplace handy. Remind yourself to use them in meetings, as problems arise, and when you are planning and conducting your work.

◈ Notes

_____

_____

_____

_____

_____

_____

_____

_____

_____

_____

_____

_____

_____

DAY 28

Finding Win/Win Solutions

Win/win is not a personality technique. It's a total paradigm of human interaction.

—Stephen Covey

How do you usually approach interactions that may involve competition, conflict, and/or negotiation? Do you:

- Fight for an outcome in which you win and someone else loses?

- Give in to a solution in which you lose and the other person wins?

- Settle for a result in which both of you lose?

- State that the solution must be one of win/win, or you will refuse to participate?

At times, any of these outcomes may be appropriate. For example, for a tennis match, a win/lose outcome is a given. It is the nature of the activity. In a situation in which you want to accommodate someone else, you may select a lose/win outcome. Sometimes, a win/win solution is appropriate. The best choice depends on the situation, and your challenge is to know which orientation is best in your situation.

However, according to Covey (1989), most situations "are part of an interdependent reality, and win/win is really the only viable alternative" (p. 211). So, if win/win (what some are now calling "gain/gain") is the most desirable paradigm for most circumstances, what does this require? Integrating a paradigm of win/win requires three character traits: integrity, maturity, and an orientation of abundance mentality (Covey, 1989). *Integrity* is the value placed on self—knowing one's values and making and keeping commitments. *Maturity* is "the balance between courage and consideration" for others (p. 217). *Abundance mentality* is an orientation to the notion that there is more than enough to go around. Lacking an abundance mentality results in seeing everything as a "zero sum" game. If this is the case, you see resources as limited and feel you must compete with others to get as much as possible for yourself or your programs. To engage in synergistic partnership requires that both parties value sharing their resources toward the greater good.

Operating out of a win/win paradigm seems easy, maybe even simplistic. In reality, it is actually very complex. Most people tend to think in "either/or" terms, and "both/and" thinking is more difficult. Ask yourself what you have to gain from a situation. What do others have to gain? What does anyone have to lose? Is there a way to minimize the loss and maximize the gain?

◈ Reflection

Think of a recent situation you were in that could have resulted in someone losing and someone winning. What was your position? If you operated from a win/win orientation, what difference did it make? If you did not, how might the outcome have been different if you had? What benefits do you see to integrating a win/win approach to working with others?

Think about a problem that you are now facing, especially a difficult one for which you can envision only a win/lose solution. Maybe budget cuts are forcing you to consider eliminating certain activities. What people share a stake in solving this problem? What conditions are needed to pull these people together and have a productive discussion focused on how to find a win/win solution?

◈ Notes

_____

_____

_____

_____

_____

_____

_____

DAY 29
Modeling Leadership

The best way we can contribute to a culture of integrity in the work-place is to speak and act with integrity ourselves.

—Roland Barth

Each day, leaders perform thousands of symbolic acts that, regardless of their size, ripple through organizations and have profound effects. The behavior of leaders is always being observed and interpreted.

Sometimes, this communication is conscious and intentional. More often, however, it is unconscious and unintentional. Here are some of the different ways leaders communicate:

- Body language (gestures, posture, touching, standing, facial expressions)
- Physical presence, including dress
- Ability and willingness to listen
- Accessibility and openness
- Words (written and spoken)
- Behavior (has a vision, walks the talk, uses good judgment, communicates with the right people)

Organizations need leaders who send clear, coherent, consistent, and appropriate messages. If leaders are vague, inconsistent, or noncommittal, followers are likely to be confused and lose connection with the leader and the organization's vision and mission.

By paying undue attention to the medium through which they communicate, leaders run the risk of focusing on style more than on substance. In reality, "There is no perceived substance without symbols" (Peters, 1987, p. 420). People build trust and credibility through observing leaders' behavior—not by reading their policy documents.

◈ Reflection

Use the previous list to consider how you model leadership. Think of the ways you communicate. Are you readily accessible? Do you have a strong physical presence? Do you have a vision? Are you a good listener? Is there congruity between your words and actions? How can you strengthen your communication skills as a leader?

◈ Notes

_____

_____

_____

_____

_____

_____

_____

_____

_____

_____

_____

DAY 30

Principle-Centered Leaders

Example is leadership.
—Albert Schweitzer

What does it mean to be a principle-centered leader?

According to Stephen Covey (1996), principle-centered leaders model such basic principles as fairness, equity, justice, honesty, trust, integrity, and service. These principles are touchstones, keeping the leader grounded in what is right to do. Principle-centered leaders demonstrate eight unique characteristics that reflect how they take care of themselves and others. According to Covey (1996), principle-centered leaders:

1. Are continually learning

2. Are service oriented

3. Radiate positive energy

4. Believe in other people

5. Lead balanced lives

6. See life as an adventure

7. Are synergistic

8. Exercise for self-renewal (physically, mentally, emotionally, and spiritually) (pp. 33–38)

◈ Reflection

What are your basic principles, and how do they shape who you are and what you do as a leader?

Consider the eight unique characteristics of principle-centered leaders. On a scale of 1 (poor) to 10 (excellent), how would you rate yourself and the other leaders in your organization on each of the dimensions? Which one or two of these characteristics do you want to enhance in your own life?

◈ Notes

DAY 31
Doing the Right Thing

You may encounter many defeats, but you must not be defeated. In fact, it may be necessary to encounter the defeats, so you can know who you are, what you can rise from, how you can still come out of it.

—Maya Angelou

How do you know you are doing the right thing?

This is a question that haunts leaders. They often have to take action without all the answers and without all the resources and support they need. Sometimes they are subject to criticism and have self-doubt, yet have to press on.

Reflection on what you are doing and why can be very helpful in addressing criticism and resolving doubt. Here are questions that can guide you to assess whether you are doing the right thing in your leadership role:

• Are factors in place that will enable your leadership efforts to be successful? Is your vision clear? Do you have a clear moral purpose? Do you have sufficient resources—both material and human? Is the timing right?

• Are you doing it because it needs to be done for your clients and organization or because it is good for you? Jim Collins (2001) found those companies that achieved great results were led by humble leaders who focused on what the organization needed over their own needs and advancement.

• Is your plan based on best practice? Have you and your team consulted the research and asked others with more experience to inform your thinking? Can you defend your decision based on research and informed professional judgment?

• Do you have sufficient support to accomplish your plan? Throughout history individuals have accomplished remarkable feats alone, but the likelihood of a single person transforming an entire organization is slim. The existing system is set up in a way that makes that very difficult to happen. Therefore, before you can be successful, you need to have a strong base of support.

◈ Reflection

Are you sure that you are doing the right things? Are you having doubt about actions you are trying to take in your organization? If so, what is the source of the doubt? Review the preceding questions. Are any of these areas you need to address?

Feedback from peers, supervisors, and subordinates can provide great insight into whether you are doing the right things. Ask for regular feedback from people around you. You can do this informally by asking a few people after a meeting to give you some feedback and/or sending out an e-mail to a small number of colleagues and ask them to make a list of your strengths and the areas they think need to be enhanced. Discuss what you learn with your coworkers and, if appropriate, be willing to make changes in your plan and actions.

🔷 Notes

_____

_____

_____

_____

_____

_____

_____

_____

_____

Bibliography

Bybee, R. W. (1993). *Reforming science education: Social perspectives and personal reflections.* New York: Teachers College Press.

Collins, J. (2001). *From good to great.* New York: HarperCollins.

Conner, D. R. (1993). *Managing at the speed of change.* New York: Villard Books.

Conner, D. R. (1998). *Leading at the edge of chaos.* New York: Wiley.

Covey, S. R. (1989). *The 7 habits of highly effective people.* New York: Simon & Schuster.

Covey, S. R. (1990). *Principle-centered leadership.* London: Simon & Schuster.

DuFour, R., & Eaker, R. (1998). *Professional learning communities at work.* Bloomington, IN: National Education Service and Alexandria, VA: Association for Supervision and Curriculum Development.

DuFour, R., DuFour, R., Eaker, R., & Karhanek, G. (2004). *Whatever it takes: How professional learning communities respond when kids don't learn.* Bloomington, IN: National Educational Service.

Ellis, D. (2002). *Falling awake: Creating the life of your dreams.* Rapid City, SD: Breakthrough Enterprises.

Fullan, M. (2001). *Leading in a culture of change.* San Francisco: Jossey-Bass.

Fullan, M. (2003). *The moral imperative of school leadership.* Thousand Oaks, CA: Corwin.

Gibb, B. (n.d.). *Classical bureaucracy and high performance system choices.* (unpublished instrument).

Goleman, D. (1995). *Emotional intelligence: Why it can matter more than IQ.* New York: Bantam Books.

Goleman, D., Boyatzis, R., & McKee, A. (2002). *Primal leadership.* Boston: Harvard Business School Press.

Kouzes, J. M., & Posner, B. Z. (2002). *The leadership challenge.* San Francisco: Jossey Bass.

Lambert, L. (1998). *Building leadership capacity in schools.* Alexandria, VA: Association for Supervision and Curriculum Development.

Lewin, R., & Regine, B. (2000). *The soul at work.* New York: Simon & Schuster.

Love, N. (2002). *Using data/getting results: Collaborative inquiry for school-based mathematics and science reform.* Norwood, MA: Christopher-Gordon.

Murphy, J., & Datnow, A. (2002). *Leadership lessons from comprehensive school reforms.* Thousand Oaks, CA: Corwin.

Myers, I. B., McCaulley, M. H., Quenk, N. L., & Hammer, A. L. (1998). *MBTI manual.* Palo Alto, CA: Consulting Psychologists Press.

Peters, T. (1987). *Thriving on chaos: Handbook for a management revolution.* New York: Knopf.

Ross, R., Smith, B., & Roberts, C. (1994). The team learning wheel. In P. Senge et al., *The fifth discipline fieldbook: Strategies and tools for building a learning organization* (pp. 59–64). New York: Doubleday.

Scholtes, P. (1998). *The leader's handbook.* New York: McGraw Hill.

Senge, P. M. (1990). *The fifth discipline.* New York: Doubleday.

Senge, P. M., Kleiner, A., Roberts, C., Ross, R. B., & Smith, B. J., (1994). *The fifth discipline fieldbook: Strageties and tools for building a learning organization.* New York: Doubleday.

Stein, S., & Book, H. (2000). *The E.Q. edge.* Toronto: Stoddart.

Terry, R. (2001). *The seven zones for leadership: Acting authentically in stability and chaos.* Palo Alto, CA: Davies-Black.

von Oech, R. (1992). *Creative whack pack.* Stamford, CT: U.S. Games Systems.

Waters, T., Marzano, R. J., & McNulty, B. (2002). *Balanced leadership: What 30 years of research tells us about the effect of leadership on student achievement.* Aurora, CO: Mid-Continent Regional Educational Lab.

Wheatley, M. (2002). *Turning to one another: Simple conversations to restore hope to the future.* San Francisco: Berrett-Koehler.

Book Two

▧ Leading Change

Book Two is a collection of thoughts and inspirations on leading change efforts. Often, the principal role of the leader is to recognize that change is needed, design the best map for change, and engage others in the journey. These 31 contemplations contain information about current research and practice on leading change in organizations.

The contemplations explore a number of key questions about change. How does change occur in an organization? Where do changes originate? Why do people experience the same change differently? What are the stages of change? How does one plan for change? What factors in our society contribute to the increasing rate of change? In any major change effort, what aspects of an organization need to remain stable? What motivates people to change? What are the roles of vision, mission, and goals in a change initiative?

And the questions continue. Why is it important to grieve what is lost when a change occurs? Why is resistance to change a natural phenomenon, and how can it be useful in guiding a change effort? Who should be involved in a major change effort? Why is an organization's change history important in determining the success of a current change initiative? Is it possible to determine an organization's readiness for change? What is the leader's role in modeling behaviors that support change? How do leaders protect themselves from burnout during intense change initiatives?

The questions are grouped around four major themes:

- What is organizational change, and how do we approach it?
- What is necessary for a successful change effort?
- What are the challenges of leading a change effort?
- What are the roles of a leader in a change initiative?

These themes are interwoven throughout the contemplations for Days 1 through 31 in Book Two.

DAY 1
Change as a Process

Change is a process, not an event.
—Gene Hall and Shirley Hord

What is the difference between an event and a process? An event is a one-time occurrence. It happens, and it is over and done with. In contrast, a process is ongoing. It takes place over time and evolves.

How do people treat change as a one-time event? The following are some typical illustrations:

- Send out a memo saying that from this point on, this is how things will be done

- Invest in a new program and expect that people will automatically be able to use it

- Send people off for training and expect them to immediately behave differently

- Enact a new policy or practice and then announce it to the staff

- Offer people professional development with the expectation that they will successfully help others

- Involve only a small number of people in making the change instead of a more broadly based group of stakeholders

- Expect to see immediate results from a change initiative

When people treat change as an event, it is doomed to fail. Unless the change is one of minimal consequence, it simply won't happen. What is different when people see change as a process? They do the following:

- Involve the people affected by the change in planning for and leading the change

- Account for the impact of change on the people involved

- Know that any significant change takes time and plan accordingly

- Employ professional development over time to ensure that people acquire the right knowledge and skills to implement the change

- Set realistic expectations for implementation

- Build a culture of support for the change that avoids blaming people for past mistakes

- Apply a monitoring procedure to track key benchmark events

Viewing change as a process increases the likelihood of obtaining the desired results.

◈ Reflection

Recall one or more examples in your organization in which change was treated as an event. How did that occur? What was the end result? How did people feel about what happened?

Are there examples from your organization in which change was treated as a process? What was different?

As a leader, what actions can you take that model change as a process rather than as an event?

◈ Notes

_____

_____

_____

_____

_____

_____

DAY 2

Change Happens in People First

Real change begins with the simple act of people talking about what they care about . . . and then the world begins to change.

—Margaret Wheatley

It is very easy to refer to an organization as an entity separate from its people. We talk about how an organization fails to value individual initiative. Or we may discuss how resistant it is to change. We treat the institution as if it were a being in and of itself.

In reality, every organization is the sum total of the people who work there each day and the structures—policies, practices, and culture—that organize them. When we say that our organization fails to value individual initiative or is resistant to change, we are really talking about key individuals and/or the organizational policies, practices, or culture that these key individuals support.

That is why change fails in organizations unless we focus on people as well as on the change itself. Paying more attention to the change than to the people making the change dooms any initiative. "Since change is made by individuals, their personal satisfactions, frustrations, concerns, motivations, and perceptions all contribute to the success or failure of a change initiative" (Loucks-Horsley & Stiegelbauer, 1991, p. 18).

◈ Reflection

Think of two or three times when you and your colleagues may have talked about your organization as if it were a separate entity apart from all who work there.

In these instances, what were you really referring to? Was it a specific person? Was it about some organizational policy or practice that you thought was unfair or outdated?

What might happen if, instead of crediting a separate identity to your organization, you more accurately pinpointed the people or aspects you had in mind?

◈ Notes

DAY 3
The Impact of Change

Whether people perceive a change as positive or negative depends not only on the actual outcomes of the change, but also on the degree of influence they believe they exert in the situation.

—Daryl Conner

Different people perceive change differently.

And the same change can affect people very differently. For some, the change may have little impact. For others, the impact may be great. Factors such as prior experience, level of knowledge and skill, individual resiliency, and the degree of influence a person has can affect how he or she experiences a change.

Here is an example. Which of the following would be hardest for you to do? Easiest?

- Move to a rural area

- Relocate to midtown of a large city

- Move to a foreign country

- Sell your house to buy a different home in the same neighborhood

All things being equal, most people would probably say that remaining in the same neighborhood would be easiest for them. But then, things are never equal when decisions about events such as those listed must be made. Some people feel very comfortable moving to a rural area or to the heart of a major metropolis, especially if that is where they grew up. A military family that once lived in Japan might welcome a return. People's prior experiences greatly influence how they approach change. Usually, the greater the familiarity and comfort with a new situation, the greater the sense of control people feel.

If the impact of the change on individuals is small or slight, implementing the change is often a simple matter. For example, filling out a different time sheet or using a new procedure for ordering supplies are minor things for most people.

But if the change has a significant potential impact—especially if it affects people's self-confidence, their span of control, their comfort, or their competence—then expect resistance. With rare exceptions, it is human nature to resist anything that has a major impact on us—even something we really desire.

Recognize, too, that individual reactions to a change effort may in part be related to race, ethnicity, gender, disability, or life circumstances. For example, an organizational move may affect one ethnic or racial group more than another if the move is to an area where there are few members of their group.

Or if a change requires extensive professional development, sessions may need to be scheduled at different times to accommodate people with small children. As a leader, you must be alert to how different people are responding to a change initiative, and address their concerns to help them move ahead with the change effort.

▨ Reflection

Think of a change effort in your organization that you have experienced. Recall how individuals responded to that change:

• Did some people implement the change with seemingly little effort? Were there any commonalties among these individuals?

• Did some people experience more difficulty? If so, did the change affect their competence, control, comfort, and/or confidence?

• Did race, ethnicity, gender, disability, or life circumstances affect how people reacted to the change? If so, how?

Was the change successfully implemented or not? Why or why not? Can you relate success or failure to how different people responded to the change?

▨ Notes

_____

_____

_____

_____

_____

DAY 4

Moving Through the Stages of Change–Concerns

There is still and will always be a critical place for consideration of the individual in the change process.

—Susan Loucks-Horsley and Suzanne Stiegelbauer

Everyone involved in a change has a somewhat different set of perceptions, expectations, feelings, motivations, and frustration points that evolve over time. We call these concerns. These concerns need to be addressed throughout the change process or people will fail to fully implement the new initiative.

The Concerns-Based Adoption Model (CBAM; Hall & Hord, 2001) provides tools to assess people's concerns about change in a way that enables leaders to know, and even predict, what concerns people have and to respond appropriately.

The concerns model delineates seven stages that people move through as they implement a change (see Table 2.1). Response to the change is developmental in nature; although people may differ in the pace at which they move through these stages, their concerns at each stage are similar.

Table 2.1   The Concerns-Based Adoption Model: Stages of Concern

Stages	Expressions of Typical Concerns
VI: Refocusing	I have some ideas about something that would work even better.
V: Collaboration	How can I relate what I am doing to what others are doing?
IV: Consequence	How is my use affecting learners? How can I refine it to have more impact?
III: Management	I seem to be spending all my time getting materials ready.
II: Personal	How will using it affect me?
I: Informational	I would like to know more about it.
0: Awareness	I am not concerned about it.

SOURCE: From Gene E. Hall, Shirley M. Hord, *Implementing Change: Patterns, Principles, and Potholes* © 2001 by Pearson Education. Reprinted by permission of publisher, Allyn & Bacon, Boston, MA.

The research on the model has revealed how people grow and develop through the stages. For example, individuals with limited experiences related to the change are likely to express concerns at Stages 0, I, or II (awareness, informational, or personal). As they become more involved and start using the practices associated with the change effort, their concerns are likely to be at Stage III (management). As they gain confidence and start noticing their impact on learners, their concerns may move to Stage IV (consequences). With experience, their concerns may shift to wanting to collaborate (Stage V) or searching for better approaches (Stage VI). Levels 0, I, and II are concerns that are focused on *self*; Level III is focused on *task*; and Levels IV, V, and VI are concerns about *impact*.

Thus, the model predicts the development of individuals within a group and enables us to assess where a group is at any moment. Knowing where people are enables the leaders of any change effort to target their interventions more effectively. For example, there is no point in focusing on use and management issues when the group isn't even familiar enough with the proposed change to identify what management issues they might encounter.

◈ Reflection

Think about a change initiative in your organization.

Are you aware of the different concerns people have about using the initiative? Do they encompass the entire continuum described, or are they concentrated in the self, task, or impact levels? How is the support you are providing directly related to people's specific stages of concern?

How can the information about the CBAM help you in leading your change effort?

◈ Notes

_____

_____

_____

_____

_____

DAY 5

Moving Through
the Stages of Change–Behavior

They always say time changes things, but you actually have to change them yourself.

—Andy Warhol

The Concerns-Based Adoption Model (Hall & Hord, 2001) delineates the levels of use that individuals typically go through in implementing an innovation. This model lists seven levels of use and common behaviors associated with each level (see Table 2.2).

Obviously, for any organization to change, the individuals who implement the change effort must change, and their leaders must support them in this process and often make the change themselves. Leaders must identify the level of use of each user in the change process and supply relevant support to match their levels.

Table 2.2   The Concerns-Based Adoption Model: Levels of Use and Behavioral Indices

Levels of Use	Behavioral Indices
VI: Renewal	The user is seeking more effective alternatives to the established use of the innovation.
V: Integration	The user is making deliberate efforts to coordinate with others in using the innovation.
IVB: Refinement	The user is making changes to enhance outcomes.
IVA: Routine	The user is making few or no changes and has an established pattern of use.
III: Mechanical	The user is using the innovation in a poorly coordinated manner and is making user-oriented changes.
II: Preparation	The user is preparing to use the innovation.
I: Orientation	The user is seeking out information about the innovation.
0: Non-use	No action is being taken with respect to the innovation.

SOURCE: From Gene E. Hall, Shirley M. Hord, *Implementing Change: Patterns, Principles, and Potholes* © 2001 by Pearson Education. Reprinted by permission of publisher, Allyn & Bacon, Boston, MA.

◈ Reflection

Go back to the organizational change effort that you recalled for the previous day's contemplation and answer the following questions, this time thinking about the levels of use:

• What level of use do you think most people are at now? Are they in preparation—just starting to use the innovation? Or, have they reached higher levels of use?

• Given this knowledge of the levels through which individuals move, what might you do differently in leading your next change initiative? How can you make sure the assistance you provide is directly tied to what the user needs?

◈ Notes

_____

_____

_____

_____

_____

_____

_____

_____

DAY 6

Using Data to Guide Change Efforts

Providing people with data before asking for their opinions and ideas . . . leads to different responses and outcomes. Possession of such information frequently requires individuals to reexamine their assumptions.

—Shirley D. McCune

If you are a seasoned leader and change agent, think back to earlier days in your career. Did you collect data to inform your decisions? If so, what data did you collect? Did you use the data? If so, in what ways? If you collected and used multiple data sources in the past, you are the exception rather than the rule.

One of the basic concepts of effective change leadership is data-based decision making. It helps you to pinpoint problems and consider alternative solutions. For example, if you know that the students who score below the 50th percentile in reading typically do not attend the district's preschool program, you may want to increase participation in the preschool program. However, because there are other variables that may be contributing to the students' lower performance, you can't conclude that enrollment in the program alone will produce results. You will want to explore other interventions, such as strengthening the reading program in the early grades and/or working with preschool parents on reading readiness strategies. Gathering additional data will help you to know which of these interventions are contributing to the achievement of the desired result.

In addition to knowing what actions to take, data reveal how your change initiative is progressing and what you need to do differently to stay on target. In the example, monitoring the number and type of students actually enrolled in the preschool program tells you whether your recruiting efforts are effective.

One of the essential components of change management is setting up information systems for decision making. Data are collected and analyzed prior to and after decision making. This enables all stakeholders to have the same information base. Such a database needs to exist at the organizational level as well as at the unit or departmental level because different decisions are made at different levels.

◈ Reflection

As a leader, consider your uses for data:

• Do you model the use of data for decision making in any change initiative that your organization undertakes? If so, how? If not, why not?

• Do you base your decisions on data and then monitor to check the results of your actions?

• What data do you find particularly helpful? Do you collect data that you really don't need?

• Do you "cast a wide net" with data collection to ensure that you gather information about the issue from a variety of perspectives?

• What data would you like to have that aren't available right now?

• Are the data accurate? Timely? In a form that is user-friendly?

If your organization does not use data in initiating and tracking change efforts, what can you do to promote the application of data-based decision making?

◈ Notes

_____

_____

_____

_____

_____

_____

_____

DAY 7

Change as Continuous Improvement

Change is a double-edged sword. Its relentless pace these days runs us off our feet. Yet when things are unsettled, we can find new ways to move ahead and to create breakthroughs not possible in stagnant societies.

—Michael Fullan

The pace of change is so great these days that organizations are continuously bombarded with one change after another. The concept of continuous improvement used to be an ideal, something that the most effective organizations strived for. Today continuous improvement is necessary for survival. Organizations that move through a loop of action-reflection-action create a continuous enhancement of culture and performance.

If organizations engage in continuous improvement, people will come to see change as a normal component of organizational life. They will regard the everyday state of their organizational and personal lives as being "permanent white water" (Vaill, 1992). A continuous improvement perspective may help to create an orientation of "polishing the stone" rather than repairing a defect.

One approach to continuous improvement is the Plan-Do-Check-Act (P-D-C-A) cycle (Senge, Kleiner, Roberts, Ross, Roth, & Smith, 1999), from the total quality management model. This approach provides a vehicle for carrying out the overall plan for a change effort, from initiation to implementation to institutionalization. In the "Plan" phase, the organization collects and analyzes data, determines the vision and/or desired outcomes, and creates an initial plan and actions. In the "Do" phase, the organization prepares people, builds the supportive environment, and implements the plan. The "Check" phase is for examining results and methods. In the "Act" phase, the organization takes appropriate actions to improve, maintain, or correct the plan and actions. Repeating this cycle results in a well-managed process and supports the concept of continuous improvement.

If change is inevitable and can be managed (as long as leaders remain flexible and in tune with the complexities and changing circumstances along the way), people are more likely to feel some degree of control instead of experiencing negative reactions, such as anger, confusion, or frustration. And if they believe that they possess some measure of control, they are more likely to support the change (Block, 1991), and a culture of continuous improvement is more likely to become a reality.

◈ Reflection

What have you done (or can you do) to promote a broader view of change as a process of continuous improvement that can be built into the culture of your organization? How are you helping everyone participate in continuous improvement of programs and practices?

◈ Notes

_____

_____

_____

_____

_____

_____

_____

_____

_____

_____

DAY 8

Complexity of Change

The more complex society gets, the more sophisticated leadership must become.

—Michael Fullan

Change in all aspects of society, including education, now proceeds at a startling rate and with a complexity that is unknown in the history of civilization.

Daryl Conner (1993, p. 39) identifies seven factors that explain why change in today's world is so complex and rapid:

1. Faster communication and knowledge acquisition

2. A growing world population

3. Increasing interdependence and competition

4. Limited resources

5. Diversified political and religious ideologies

6. Constant transitions of power

7. Ecological distress

Most of these factors have their counterparts in the educational system: the rapid rate at which knowledge is changing, along with continuous improvements in information technology; the increasing diversity of the populations served by schools; the growing awareness of the interrelatedness of schools and the communities in which they exist; tight resources; the advocacy efforts of special interest groups; and the rapid turnover of school and district staff. Each of these factors creates change independently of and in conjunction with the others.

Fullan (1993) describes an educational system that is trying to respond to this speed and complexity:

> School districts and schools are in the business of implementing a bewildering array of multiple innovations and policies simultaneously. Moreover, restructuring reforms are so multifaceted and complex that solutions for particular settings cannot be known in advance. If one tries to match the complexity of the situation with complex implementation plans, the process becomes unwieldy, cumbersome and usually wrong. (p. 24)

This illustrates why change must be regarded as a journey and not a blueprint.

There are too many unknowns and unknowables; it may be impossible to determine the solution in advance. There are always unexpected events; rarely can they be fully predicted (that is why they're unexpected).

Change is a journey marked by detours, dead ends, and cloverleafs, with an occasional stretch of clear motoring along the way. In extreme cases, even the original destination may change. This in no way obviates the need for an overall plan or the use of a process like the P-D-C-A cycle. (See Day 7 of this book.) You must recognize your destination as you near it. The repeated application of P-D-C-A will help you reach your target.

◈ Reflection

How are Conner's seven factors relevant to the rate and complexity of change in your organization? Which are the most significant? Are there other factors that contribute to the rate and complexity of change that you experience?

Think about some change effort or perhaps a complex project that you have observed in your organization. Did things always go according to plan? For example:

• What events happened that were planned and accounted for in advance?

• What events happened that were unanticipated?

• Was the change effort or project flexible enough to handle the unexpected?

• Was it ultimately successful? If so, what factors contributed to its success?

• What lessons did the organization learn from the change? How was this understanding incorporated into subsequent efforts?

How can you help your organization better understand change as a journey that requires great flexibility and ongoing assessment?

◈ Notes

DAY 9

Balancing Constants and Change

The art of progress is to preserve order amid change and to preserve change amid order.

—Alfred North Whitehead

Change, change, change! We hear that word so much these days. So much, in fact, that we may forget that change is just one side in one of the fundamental dichotomies of life. The other choice is to stay the same. As discussed in Book One, Day 24, one paradox leaders must balance is "initiating change while maintaining continuity."

In many change efforts, the parts that stay the same are overlooked. The entire focus is on the changes going on—not the elements that remain stable, stationary, and strong in the midst of change.

Dichotomies (centralization versus decentralization, holding on versus letting go, and staying the same versus changing) are best viewed as "both/ands" rather than "either/ors."

In any successful change effort, considerable attention needs to be given to what remains constant. Without this balanced view, the daunting perception of change can overwhelm a system and the people in it.

So, how do you balance staying the same and changing in an organization? You deliberately and thoughtfully designate some things that will not change during a certain period. For example, your school will implement a new curriculum in mathematics and science for K–6 over the next three years, but the reading and social studies curricula will remain stable. Balance can also be achieved by conducting a change priority inventory (Kaser & Horsley, 1998a), so that competing change initiatives do not negate each other in their struggle for resources. A change inventory does the following: documents how many people are affected by the change and who they are; estimates the impact and potential outcomes of the change; provides a timeline for full implementation of the change; and lists all of the resource requirements. Such an inventory can identify what is not being changed along with the changes that are planned.

The areas of stability need to be highlighted in written and oral communications and supported by leaders in the organization. This assures the staff that the leadership is committed to balanced change and to keeping what is good and what works well within the organization. For example, one of the authors recently met a principal new to her school. Her first act as principal was to interview each teacher, asking two questions: (1) What are the three things that I should not "touch" or consider changing? and (2) What are your top three priorities for things that need to change to enhance teaching and learning in this school? The principal's communication with each teacher and the targeted questions clearly sent the message that she was intent on keeping what worked well and balancing change with stability.

🔷 Reflection

Jot down some of the change initiatives going on in your organization. Can you balance each change effort with some parallel aspect of your organization that is remaining stable? If you can't, people are likely to feel overwhelmed by all the changes.

If your organization is not emphasizing stability sufficiently to balance the desired change, what can you do?

🔷 Notes

_____

_____

_____

_____

_____

_____

_____

DAY 10
Recognizing Mental Models

The inertia of deeply entrenched mental models can overwhelm even the best systemic insights.

—Peter Senge

Another requirement for an organization to respond successfully to change is awareness of what Senge (1990) calls *mental models*. Mental models run the gamut from simple generalizations or stereotypes about people and things to complex belief systems about how the world works. Senge believes that these mental models influence how we think and act.

One common example of a firmly entrenched mental model or belief is the emphasis in education on effort rather than result. Historically, educators have looked upon their role as that of providing education; whether children and youth actually acquired an education was primarily the students' responsibility since they had been given the opportunity to learn. However, today the emphasis has shifted to results. If students are not learning, then what do educators need to do differently to help all children succeed? The primary accountability is now with the school.

Another mental model being challenged by contemporary thought is that of leadership. Rather than leadership being vested only in the midlevel and top management of an organization (the firmly entrenched model again), we are now regarding all staff as having certain leadership responsibilities. But if that is the case, we have to set up different structures in our organizations to accommodate, support, and encourage this broader concept of leadership. Old structures don't mesh with the new mental model.

We act on the basis of our mental models continually, so it is important to surface them in conversations and develop a shared awareness of what they are. When encountering a problem, ask yourself, "What about my beliefs or mental model is contributing to this problem?" When we decide, we act on our assumptions; and the assumptions usually remain implicit. Making our assumptions or mental models explicit helps us better understand why we make the choices we make and can lead to great insights. In turn, those insights can result in better communication and more effective decision making and problem solving.

◈ Reflection

Can you identify some of the basic mental models you and other individuals in your organization hold? Perhaps start with views of leadership. What are the assumptions you and others hold about who should be a leader and what traits leaders should possess?

What are some of the mental models you and others hold about your organization? Do you assume all can succeed, or do you think some must fail? Do you believe that individuals must have certain prerequisites or follow a certain path to be successful? Do you view your organization as impervious to change? What could happen if you changed your mental models? How might changing a mental model affect the outcome of a change initiative?

◈ Notes

_____

_____

_____

_____

_____

_____

_____

_____

_____

DAY 11

Shared Vision

Leadership isn't about imposing the leader's solo dream; it's about developing a shared sense of destiny.

—James M. Kouzes and Barry Z. Posner

What's the desired result of an organizational change effort, and who decides it?

The desired result, or shared vision, doesn't emerge from a small group effort or by upper-level managers issuing a statement that others are expected to follow. As discussed in Book One, Day 6, a true vision is never imposed. It evolves through people having a similar picture of what they want and knowing that they can achieve this goal most effectively by their collective, not individual, actions.

Reaching shared vision of the change required and how it will contribute to your success starts with individuals crafting their personal visions. "If people don't have their own vision, all they can do is 'sign up' for someone else's" (Senge, 1990, p. 211). It is the personal vision that motivates. People with their own personal visions can form a powerful group to create what they want for themselves and for their organization. However, the vision for your change initiative must also be aligned with your organization's overall vision. If not, the change will likely fail.

A litmus test of the power of a vision is whether people know it and live it. There are likely to be different emphases from person to person, but the similarity should be apparent. A vision fails the test when it is merely something on a piece of paper that has to be looked up.

A leader's role in leading a change effort is to help people connect the desired change to their own personal visions and to make sure these personal visions are aligned with the organization's overall vision.

◈ Reflection

Consider a change initiative in your organization that you are involved with. Does it have a compelling vision? Is it aligned with the overall organization's vision?

As a leader, what will you do with others to build a consistent vision of the change effort, including why you are making the change and how it ties to your organizational vision, mission, and goals?

Notes

_____

_____

_____

_____

_____

_____

_____

_____

_____

_____

_____

_____

_____

DAY 12

Mission and Goals

The greatest satisfaction you can find in life comes from discovering and courageously following your mission.

—Richard Barrett

What gives an organization a common sense of direction?

As the previous day's contemplation points out, a shared vision is absolutely essential for any change initiative to succeed. However, more is required.

Organizations need to be clear about their missions—who they are and what their purpose is—and how the change effort relates to and supports the mission. This is different from a vision that describes the future state or conditions an organization desires. There may also be specific goals and activities or programs appropriate to the mission that will help achieve the shared vision.

Although there is usually just one vision for either the organization or for a change initiative, different parts of an organization may have their own mission statements and goals that are aligned with the vision. In some organizations, individuals write personal mission statements that are compatible with their unit's. This results in a staff that has a common sense of direction.

For example, a school may have as part of its vision that the staff are continuous learners. This is in turn supported by a mission statement that every teacher and educational support personnel participate in ongoing professional development. Different departments may have their own goals in support of continuous learning, for example, improving questioning techniques, developing better strategies for teaching diverse students, or learning to use new assessments. However, all support the vision of the school.

For leaders, having a shared vision, clear mission, and specific goals are essential parts of change management. Together, these items serve as a compass for organizational action.

▧ Reflection

Are you clear about your mission and goals? As a leader of change, how do you communicate with others about the change effort's mission and goals?

How does the change initiative you are leading support your mission? If it is not in line with your mission, what modifications are needed?

◈ Notes

_____

_____

_____

_____

_____

_____

_____

_____

_____

_____

_____

DAY 13
Motivating Others

There is only one way under high Heaven to get anybody to do anything. Did you ever stop to think of that? Yes, just one way. And that is by making the other person want to do it. Remember, there is no other way.

—Dale Carnegie

What is motivation to change? Is it simple or complex, one dimensional or multidimensional?

What sustains motivation to achieve a goal? What keeps us going even when our chances of success seem remote?

According to Richard Barrett (1999), motivation has four dimensions: physical, emotional, mental, and spiritual. The physical and emotional dimensions are satisfied primarily by external conditions. For example, financial reward is an example of the physical component; open communication is an example of the emotional. Physical and emotional aspects can be fulfilled by either positive external incentives (for example, promotions) or negative external incentives (for example, loss of status). The efficiency of external rewards declines over time and so must be increased to remain motivational.

Although all four dimensions will motivate individuals, the most sustainable level of commitment comes when mental and spiritual needs are satisfied. The mental dimension is met through opportunities for professional and personal growth or opportunities to use new knowledge and skills to solve real problems. The spiritual dimension is met through having work that is meaningful, that matters, and that makes a difference in the world.

Commitments are sustained by *creative tension* (Fritz, 1989). Think of a stretched rubber band. One pole is your current reality: the existing state you are dissatisfied with, the state causing you to feel discomfort. The other pole is your vision: that which you want to achieve. The discrepancy between the poles creates a tension, and the natural resolution of tension is to move closer to the vision of what you want (Senge et al., 1999). If this tension is strong enough, individuals may feel compelled to persevere because "they have assimilated the vision not just consciously, but unconsciously, at a level where it changes more of their behavior." They may have a "sustained sense of energy and enthusiasm, which . . . produces some tangible results, which can then make the energy and enthusiasm stronger" (Senge, Kleiner, Roberts, Ross, & Smith, 1994, p. 195).

Reaching this level of commitment generally suggests that people have satisfied the mental and spiritual dimensions of their motivation. If not, the tension would be inadequate to support sustained action.

◈ Reflection

Think about your role in leading change. What dimensions of motivation are you addressing? Are there incentives or disincentives for people's physical and emotional needs? What opportunities exist for fulfilling the mental and spiritual needs? Are you providing professional development, and can people solve problems using their new knowledge and skill? Do they find the work meaningful? Do they have a sense of making a difference? If the rewards are more external than internal, what can you as a leader do to address the mental and spiritual aspects and strengthen commitment?

Consider the people involved in your change effort. On a scale of 1 (low) to 10 (high), how much tension do they experience between your organization's current reality and your desired state? What evidence do you have to make this determination? How do you either maintain or increase that tension? Are there any additional strategies that might enhance people's commitment to change?

◈ Notes

_____

_____

_____

_____

_____

_____

DAY 14

Planning for Change

We think in generalities, but we live in detail.
—Alfred North Whitehead

How concrete are the details regarding your change initiative? Are these details set forth in a written plan?

Are the people involved in formulating the change initiative aware of what is happening and when? Is there a timetable? Do people know what is expected of them and are they committed to carring out their roles? Have benchmarks been set to gauge progress? Are organizational supports in place for institutionalization? Are there criteria for success?

And most important, is the plan flexible? Can it be adjusted in response to unanticipated events? Is it reviewed and adjusted regularly? Are revisions to the plan communicated to others involved in the change initiative?

A component in managing successful change is having a plan for each stage. Such a plan details what steps will be taken, by whom, at what point, and to what end. A plan has the following purposes or dimensions:

- Sets forth desired outcomes

- Serves as a guide for achieving those outcomes

- Identifies the benchmarks that will be used to monitor how well the intervention is progressing

- Documents the degree of alignment that exists among the vision, missions, goals, and activities

- Serves as a means for aligning the intervention throughout the organization

A plan for any stage is not cast in stone. As change efforts evolve, the plan is revised; that is the nature of organizational change. Overall direction and guiding principles are always more important than the details. However, as each next step comes closer in time, the details become more important. Flexibility is the key. A dynamic plan continually serves as a guide for all to follow.

One final caveat: Make sure that far more energy goes into carrying out the plan than in developing it. Avoid becoming so focused on the plan that implementation does not occur.

◈ Reflection

Does your organization have a documented plan (or plans) for its change initiative? Is it a working document that the staff uses and regularly updates? Who is the custodian of the plan? Who knows about the plan and has access to it? Do evaluation and reflection activities inform revisions to the plan?

If you answered any of these questions "No," what can you do to encourage your organization to develop a working plan?

◈ Notes

_____

_____

_____

_____

_____

_____

_____

_____

DAY 15

Origins of Change

Change and improvement processes evolve and change to fit the shifting environment and what's being learned about what works and what doesn't. Both top-down and local, or bottom-up, approaches are needed. The challenge is finding the right balance.

—Jim Clemmer

How many times have you heard people (maybe even yourself) debating about whether organizational change comes from the top or the bottom and where it should actually originate? It's an age-old argument.

A typical conversation may sound something like this: "You can't impose change from the top. I don't care how many edicts leaders issue, change can't be mandated. If the people don't want to change, there are all kinds of ways to undermine any initiative. Any real change has to come from the staff—not the leaders. Let me tell you about what happened in my organization. . . ."

Another counters: "People at lower levels rarely have the power, authority, or resources to bring about any kind of major change on their own. Quit kidding yourself. Organizations can squelch a budding initiative just by firing a person or two or denying them resources. Any real change has to have the sanctions and support of leaders. Let me tell you about what happened in my organization. . . ."

And so the arguments go. If you have found yourself caught up in such discussions, vow right now that you won't repeat such a conversation. The question itself is a spurious one, posed as either/or: Change comes either from the top or from the bottom.

In reality, it is both. Both the leaders and the staff must be active players in a change initiative if it is to succeed. Either one is capable of subverting a change, so both must be working in concert to ensure success.

❧ Reflection

Think of some change effort in your organization that succeeded. What role did the leaders play? What was the staff's role? How was the change initiated? Was it lodged more in the top or the base of the organization, or was it spread across the organization? Did the leaders support the change effort? (Many change efforts fail because leaders don't provide sustained support.)

How did the staff come to implement the change effort? (Change efforts can also fail because the staff is not supported to develop the interest, knowledge, or skills to carry out the new initiative.) How were people informed? Did the change effort expand to include more people? How did this happen? What can you learn from this effort that would help you in your role of leading change?

◈ Notes

_____

_____

_____

_____

_____

_____

_____

_____

_____

_____

DAY 16

Accepting Loss

He that lacks time to mourn lacks time to mend.

—William Shakespeare

In some way, all significant change involves giving up something of your former self, and all losses must be grieved.

Whenever a major change takes place, we lose something. It may be the loss of a relationship, an office, or a lesson we loved to teach. Even if we want the change (perhaps a better relationship, a nicer office, or an improved curriculum), we still feel a loss. The loss may be a pattern of interaction, a convenient working environment, or the joy of helping others learn something important to us; or it may be the loss of that which was comfortable and familiar.

A loss that remains ungrieved keeps us anchored in the past, unable to fully commit to the present. From the work of Dr. Elisabeth Kübler-Ross (1970), we learn something about how people grieve death. She identified five stages of the grief process:

Stage 1: *Denial.* We pretend that nothing has happened. Things will be just the way they have always been. Perhaps we are having a bad dream. We'll wake up, and everything will be fine. We may enter into a robot-like stage in which we suppress our anger and become depressed. Because we are in denial, we don't tell other people. In fact, we haven't even told ourselves.

Stage 2: *Anger.* Feeling angry about a loss is normal and necessary. We may feel angry at another person, maybe even at the world. Why did this have to happen to us? Life isn't fair. Or: Why did this have to happen now? The timing is not good.

Stage 3: *Bargaining.* In this stage, we seek to make amends. What do we have to do to restore conditions to what they were? What can we trade or give up? What can we promise to do or never do again?

Stage 4: *Letting go.* This stage is the final letting go of the old. It is, in one sense, the darkness before the dawn. It may be characterized by deep sadness. It is a reflective stage in that we ask deep questions, such as "What is the meaning of this experience?" "What do I truly want for myself?" "What have I learned over the past weeks or months?" Rarely does letting go occur at a single instant. Rather, it occurs incrementally.

Stage 5: *Acceptance.* Here, we have moved beyond our emotional attachment to the loss and have relinquished our investment in the past. We are now ready to move and to accept whatever new situation is awaiting. We are reenergized and hopeful about the future.

Movement through the stages is similar to that of an organization going through systemic change. Progress is not linear, and it is possible for people to become stuck in a stage or skip a stage completely. Some may even work backward or appear to move in circles. However, for the grieving process to be most effective, grievers need—at some point—to experience each stage.

In organizations, resistance may come from losses ungrieved. According to Garmston and Wellman (1999), "Endings must be marked concretely and symbolically" (p. 248). In the absence of grieving, the staff may hold on to elements of the old and not be able to fully embrace the new.

❧ Reflection

Again, think of a major change going on in your organization. What is the loss that the staff may be feeling? Have you found ways to help people grieve that loss? If so, how? If not, what steps can you take to facilitate the process of natural grieving?

❧ Notes

_____

_____

_____

_____

_____

_____

_____

_____

DAY 17

Dealing With Disappointment

You may be disappointed if you failed, but you are doomed if you don't try.

—Beverly Sills

In spite of your good intentions and actions, you may fail in your attempts to bring about a major change in your organization. The reasons are manifold: a defeated levy, a change in top leadership, the lobbying of an opposing group. Or maybe you chose the wrong plan, or the timing was wrong. Or perhaps the loss is more personal: you didn't get the promotion, or you were given another assignment and couldn't follow through with your plans.

Failure and disappointment are inevitable. If you don't occasionally fail, you're probably not doing enough. The problem is not failing; it's knowing how to learn from your failures and move on. Learning from failures is accepting disappointment, a natural reaction to falling short of our goals; discerning what you can about the failure; and then trying again with new knowledge.

One of the first reactions to disappointments is to blame someone or something: If only she had done this or he had agreed to that, this wouldn't have happened. Blaming triggers defensiveness, even anger, and hinders a dispassionate examination of what happened and how it happened. In fact, it's better to ask questions that start with *what* and *how* rather than those that begin with *why, when,* and *who.*

Your approach to dealing with your own disappointment sets a tone for your organization. According to Cini (2004), here are five things that you can do:

1. *Don't take disappointments personally.* Perhaps analyze the situation as if it had happened to someone else. That will likely give you a different perspective.

2. *Know yourself. Especially, know your values.* Perhaps this organization is not the right place for you at this time. Perhaps you need to make a move.

3. *Take full responsibility for yourself and your actions.* Don't blame others, bad luck, bad timing, or other external factors for the failure. Acknowledge your role fully and move on.

4. *Think beyond your own situation.* How did this failure impact your colleagues and the organization as a whole?

5. *Explore this situation with your boss. You and your supervisor need to be clear on what happened.* Just as you don't want to blame others, you want to avoid being blamed, too.

◈ Reflection

Think of a time when you experienced a failure of some sort in your organization. How did you and others around you respond? Was blame cast, or were you able to dissect what happened and how it happened objectively? If finger pointing was going on, what was the effect? How did you and your organization recover?

What is your typical pattern of handling disappointment? Do you blame others or yourself? Are you clear about the difference between blaming your-self and taking responsibility for your behavior? Are you a positive role model for dealing with disappointment? What might you do differently?

◈ Notes

_____

_____

_____

_____

_____

_____

_____

DAY 18

Change and Resilience

What one has to do usually can be done.

—Eleanor Roosevelt

How well equipped are people to handle change? How do you know their potential for responding to change?

Daryl Conner (1998) sees each person as having an individual *speed of change*. He defines this as the rate at which you can move through the adaptation process with a minimum of dysfunctional behavior—the pace at which you can bounce back from the confusion caused by uncertainty and grasp the opportunities that the new environment presents (p. 189).

According to Conner, the single, most important factor that affects one's speed of change is resilience. Highly resilient individuals are able to operate at a higher speed of change than those who are less resilient.

Conner (1998) identified five characteristics that constitute resiliency:

1. *Positiveness:* Resilient individuals effectively identify opportunities in turbulent environments and have confidence in their ability to succeed.

2. *Focus:* Resilient individuals have a clear vision of what they want to achieve, and they use this as a lodestar to guide them should they become disoriented.

3. *Flexibility:* Resilient individuals draw effectively on a wide range of internal and external resources to develop creative, malleable strategies for responding to change.

4. *Organization:* Resilient individuals use structured approaches to manage ambiguity, planning, and coordinating effectively in implementing their strategies.

5. *Proactivity:* Resilient individuals act in the face of uncertainty and take calculated risks rather than seeking comfort. (p. 189)

Although these five factors are interrelated to some extent, they are separate attributes. One change initiative may draw principally from one or two factors, whereas another may tap a different factor. This led Conner (1998) to view resilience as "the ability to draw effectively on whichever characteristic, or combination of characteristics, is called for in a particular situation" (p. 193).

Conner (1998) also sees a link between resiliency and physical health. The higher the resiliency, the greater the likelihood of excellent physical health and vice versa. He has also identified a similar link between the level of resilience and leadership. Leaders in organizations are more likely to have higher levels of resilience, and those with high resilience are more likely to be leaders.

◈ Reflection

Using Conner's five factors (positiveness, focus, flexibility, organization, and proactivity) plus overall physical health, how would you rate your own resiliency? How about key staff you work with in your change effort? Which of these factors stand out?

Although resiliency is personal, it can be affected by what goes on in an organization. As a leader, what can you do to bolster people's positiveness, focus, flexibility, organization, proactivity, and overall physical health?

◈ Notes

_____

_____

_____

_____

_____

_____

_____

DAY 19

Facing Problems

Problems are our friends.
—Michael Fullan

Sounds a little scary, right? This is especially true given the complex nature of the problems that organizations and society as a whole face today. How can problems have any kind of positive connotation?

Problems in the broadest sense are inevitable. Given the increasing complexity of our society and the rapid rate of change, we are going to experience more and more problems, most of which will be complex and not easily resolved. It is our reality—whether we like it or not. If we confront our fears, we have a better chance of resolving them. Rather than trying to avoid a problem or pretend it doesn't exist, we are better off facing it directly.

It is through solving problems, often by trial and error, that we learn. As the saying goes, "No pain, no gain!" Without the problem, we would not have the learning. One of the characteristics of adaptive organizations is an acceptance of failure as inevitable and valuable. We often learn more from a failed attempt than a successful one. In today's organizations, however, failure is not carte blanche. It is balanced with accountability. What Garmston and Wellman (1999) call *failing forward* is the way people learn from their errors. In failing forward, we advance by the way we respond to a situation. Instead of reacting to the event and attempting a quick fix, we dig deeper to determine the root cause of the problem and to correct what organizational policies, programs, or practices are at the core. In that sense, problems are opportunities for us to broaden our attitudes, knowledge, and skills while moving our organizations forward.

◈ Reflection

What is the prevailing attitude in your organization toward problems? Are they ignored? Seen as troublesome interruptions? Looked on as opportunities to improve products or services and to advance knowledge in the organization?

What is your organization's attitude toward failure? Are people able and willing to take risks without fear of recrimination? Do people learn from their mistakes, and does that learning become part of the organization's common knowledge?

As a leader, what can you do to help people in your organization see problems as friends rather than enemies? What can you do to establish a climate supportive of failing forward?

◈ Notes

_____

_____

_____

_____

_____

_____

_____

_____

_____

_____

DAY 20

Neutralizing Resistance

One cannot hope to implement change without persuading people that it is necessary. This is a task of daunting proportions that must often start by challenging people's view of themselves, their performance and their clients.

—Robert Evans

Getting people to feel some sense of urgency for a major change is an art form. Lowering resistance involves increasing the tension of not supporting the change effort and reducing the tension related to trying it. Both drive behavior in the direction of the change.

What are some ways of decreasing resistance to change?

1. *Increase the tension of not supporting the change.*

   - Provide data that documents the need for the change.

   - Make it clear that all are expected to make the change.

   - Make sure that all key opinion leaders support and model the change. Ask them to garner the support of others.

2. *Decrease the tension related to trying the new way.*

   - Determine the concerns of the resisters. Are they afraid they will fail or have too little time to learn a new approach? Find out what they are worried about and respond with the appropriate intervention.

   - Help resisters make the connection between their personal visions and the organizational vision.

   - Set up a timetable that allows adequate assimilation time.

In describing what often happens in organizations, John Kotter (1996) says:

I've seen people start by building the change coalitions, by creating the change vision, or by simply making changes. But the problems of inertia and complacency always seem to catch up with them. Sometimes they quickly hit a wall, as when a lack of urgency makes it impossible to put together a powerful enough leadership team to guide the changes. Sometimes people go for years before it becomes apparent that various initiatives are flagging. (p. 49)

One way that leaders keep people out of the "complacency zone" is to identify and celebrate milestones in the implementation of the change effort. As we point out in the very first contemplation in this book, effective leaders keep attention and energy focused on the success of the change effort. They recognize and celebrate milestones, which gives people a sense of control and accomplishment.

A caution: If the degree or extent of resistance seems greater than would normally be expected, leaders should look at the change initiative itself. Perhaps it is not the appropriate initiative for the culture of your organization or circumstances. Maybe there is a better solution waiting. Knowing people's specific objections can help you determine if you need to reconsider what you are proposing.

◈ Reflection

As a leader of change, what do you do when people resist change? What are the factors that fuel their resistance? Have your strategies focused both on decreasing disincentives and increasing incentives? What is your evidence of decreasing resistance? If your change requires a long time for implementation, is there a danger of people becoming complacent? If so, how can you keep people engaged and motivated and reduce complacency?

◈ Notes

_____

_____

_____

_____

_____

_____

_____

DAY 21

Capitalizing on Resistance

Understand that resistance can be a gold mine!
—Carol Bershad and Susan Mundry

When you hear the word *resistance*, does it conjure up a positive or a negative reaction?

Most people will think negatively: that resistance is an obstacle and something to be overcome.

What would happen if you reframed the notion of resistance? What if you saw it as an indicator of where people were in relation to a change? What if you saw resistance as an opportunity for you and others to learn? How might this change your perspective?

The level of resistance to change in an organization often gives us insight into the potential impact of the change. The greater the impact of the change, the more resistance it is likely to encounter. For example, substituting one textbook for another is not likely to have great impact, and therefore minimal resistance is likely to appear. However, moving from a textbook to an activity-based curriculum is likely to have much greater impact and therefore give rise to greater resistance. Resistance is normal and natural. If there is no resistance, you can assume that the impact of change is minimal or that people are indifferent.

Understanding that resistance stems from feelings can help us delve deeper to determine the source of resistance. And once we know the source of the resistance, dealing with it becomes much easier. Here are 12 common sources of resistance divided into different categories:

Sources Related to Not Having the Ability to Change

1. Lack of knowledge and skills in the content

2. Lack of knowledge and skills in the process

Sources Related to the Lack of Willingness to Change

3. Lack of support for the change because of poor communication

4. Lack of ownership, seeing no need

5. Lack of alignment between the change and the culture of the organization

6. Lack of resources of time, materials, and/or facilities

7. Having an oppositional nature (either individuals or a group); disliking the mandated change

8. Lack of leadership or positive role models

9. Lack of trust in the system or in the leaders

Sources Related to Special Circumstances

10. Style differences that are misinterpreted as resistance

11. Having a sincere and accurate belief that the proposed change is wrong or that it is being implemented the wrong way

12. Personal reasons unrelated to the change (for example, focusing on another challenging work project or change effort, impending retirement, pregnancy, serious illness, an so on) (Kaser & Horsley, 1998b, pp. 1–2)

☒ Reflection

How much resistance do you encounter to your current change effort? Can you identify the sources of the resistance? What steps are you taking to overcome the resistance? What can other people do?

Can you think of at least one antidote for each one of the 12 sources of resistance? There are actually several for each one of the sources, so if you can come up with more than one, you are thinking in the right direction.

Here are just a few ways that leaders address resistance to change:

- Build relationships among all

- Practice communicating the negative aspects of the change as well as the positive

- Gather data about people's concerns

- Address people's concerns directly with support and assistance

- Build a shared vision of what you are trying to accomplish and how it will benefit everyone

- Communicate high expectations for everyone to make the change (Mundry & Bershad, 1998)

▤ Notes

DAY 22

Knowing Your Constituents

Unless you regularly account for all your stakeholders, your organization will likely not survive.

—Stephen Covey

Who is involved in your change effort?

It's a rare organization today that doesn't have several stakeholder groups to deal with. Take a public school, for example. In addition to employees and a governing body, there are children and youth, parents and community members, unions, businesses, other institutions such as colleges and universities, and perhaps even some special interest groups. All of these groups need to be considered in any organizational change, as they are likely to have a vested interest.

Implementing any kind of major change is so difficult that your instinct may be to limit involvement. However, ignoring some group or not keeping key people properly informed and engaged is likely to backfire and may derail your initiative later. If you only occasionally reach out to stakeholders, you are likely to raise their expectations and have them experience frustration if their involvement does not lead to change.

Covey (1992) points out that real change happens when organizations begin to problem solve around data gained from stakeholders. He recommends a "stakeholder information system—a feedback system or database on what shareholders, customers, employees, communities, suppliers, distributors, and other parties want and expect" (Covey, 1992, p. 258). He suggests that if a stakeholder information system is set up properly, data can be highly accurate as long as they are obtained "systematically, scientifically, anonymously, using random sampling of the population" (Covey, 1992, p. 258).

Here is an instance of a school administrator who failed to consider his stakeholders:

His elementary school was slated to be closed, and students would be moved to a much larger, more modern school across town. He went on record as fully supporting this decision. The school they were leaving was old, lacked a gym and adequate wiring for computers, and was not accessible to persons with disabilities. The parents were outraged. They saw the smallness and character of the old school, the individual attention it afforded children, and its proximity and community school atmosphere as benefits that far outweighed the negatives. In a public forum, the principal was shown to be out of touch with one of his most important stakeholder groups.

Using Covey's idea of establishing a stakeholder information system, how could this situation have been avoided?

◈ Reflection

Who are the stakeholders affected by the change your organization is proposing? What assumptions are you making about how they will react to the change? Have you verified your assumptions with members of the group?

How are you involving them in your reform effort? Has anyone been left out? If so, why? How will you bring them on board?

Do you have a stakeholder information system established? If not, how could you establish one?

◈ Notes

_____

_____

_____

_____

_____

_____

_____

Managing Multiple Change Efforts

Q: How can executives manage 29 change projects all at once?

A: They can't. In successful transformations, executives lead the overall effort and leave most of the managerial work and the leadership of specific activities to their subordinates.

—John P. Kotter

The nomenclature used in Book Two (that is, the use of the terms that describe change initiatives) may be misleading. Expressions such as "developing a mission" or "data-based decision making" may lead a reader to believe that change occurs in a linear fashion, one initiative at a time.

Nothing, however, could be farther from the truth. It would be rare for an organization to have a single reform effort in place. It is not uncommon for a school district, for example, to identify 50 or more changes going on at the district level.

One of the major reasons change efforts fail is that they are overshadowed and sometimes overrun by others that have more support and resources. Unless leaders attend specifically to each change effort and its relationship to the vision, mission, and goals of the organization, some inevitably stave off others. *Attending* means (1) knowing what resources each reform effort needs to be successful and delivering them, and/or (2) prioritizing the various change efforts so that each has a different ranking over a specific period of time. Such determinations cannot be haphazard.

Attending to each change effort independently is critical for another reason. Each has its own goals, staffing, resource requirements, and timetable. Sponsors and supporters, including stakeholders, are likely to be different. The impact of the change varies from one initiative to another; and it is the impact of change on people that determines how easy or difficult implementation will be. If you are gathering data about your change effort, they must be collected separately for each initiative so that you understand the particulars for each one.

Just as you need to treat each change initiative individually, you need to see each in relation to the others and support appropriate coordination and integration. A major organizational paradox exists: treating each change effort individually while seeing each as part of a larger whole. As a leader, you need to keep the big picture in mind, looking across the different initiatives to note overlap and meeting coordination and integration needs.

◈ Reflection

Make a list of the changes you have initiated or implemented this year. (You might ask a colleague to do the same thing and then compare your lists.) How many did you come up with? Were you surprised by the number? Why?

Now consider who is involved in these initiatives. Do you see any patterns? Are some people overburdened? Are some left out? Do any of these change efforts compete with each other for resources? Are any in danger of failing? If so, what can you do to salvage change initiatives that are threatened?

Is each change effort being treated independently and at the same time being seen as part of a larger whole? If not, what can you do to make sure that each change initiative is seen from this dual perspective? Can you identify linkages between and among the various change efforts?

Are the change efforts aligned with the organization's vision, mission, and goals and with each other?

◈ Notes

_____

_____

_____

_____

_____

_____

_____

_____

DAY 24

Systems Thinking

Today, systems thinking is needed more than ever because we are becoming overwhelmed by complexity.

—Peter Senge

What is systems thinking, and how does it relate to organizational change?

Systems thinking is a particular form of analysis that, rather than breaking a problem down into discrete components, helps people examine the big picture, looking for interrelationships among interactions, causes, and effects. Developed by Jay Forrester at MIT in 1956, the ideas were not widely used until the expansion of total quality management in the United States and Peter Senge's identification of systems thinking as the missing ingredient for effective organizations in the 1990s.

In his book *The Fifth Discipline*, Peter Senge (1990) outlines 11 "laws" that are characteristic of systems thinking. Three of these are especially relevant to bringing about change in organizations:

1. *"Today's problems come from yesterday's 'solutions'"* (p. 57). Although we usually hope that solving a problem takes care of a situation, in reality, solving one problem often creates another. For example, the high school that instituted a high minimum grade point average for all athletes found that its dropout rate increased. Instead of motivating students to study harder and get good grades, the rule had the effect of pushing a certain group of students off the teams and out the door. Solving problems in a system without simply transferring a problem from one part of the system to another is a delicate business.

2. *"Cause and effect are not closely related in time and space"* (p. 63). In simple situations, seeing a direct and timely relationship between cause and effect is common. For example, children learn very quickly that if they don't share their toys and play nicely, they are likely to be removed from their play group. But direct cause-and-effect relationships like these are uncommon in complex systems such as our organizations. For example, in the high school example just given, cause and effect were not what this well-intended group of educators expected them to be.

3. *"Small changes can produce big results—but the areas of highest leverage are often the least obvious"* (p. 63). In systems thinking, the most obvious solutions often don't work. Setting a grade point average cutoff for participation is the most obvious solution for dealing with student athletes who are not

doing well academically. The only problem is that it doesn't have the desired effect (pp. 57–67). A powerful example of a small change that led to a dynamic impact is that of Rosa Parks, in 1955, in Montgomery, Alabama. She refused to give up her seat for a white man and move to the back of the bus. Her act sparked the civil rights movement across the United States.

We know from chaos theory that often some small, insignificant action strategically placed can result in significant and lasting improvements. These are called *high-leverage* changes. The problem with such changes is that they are not obvious and not closely connected in time and space to the problem at hand.

Although difficult, it is possible to find high-leverage changes. Senge (1990) recommends that learning to see the underlying structures, patterns, and assumptions that drive thinking and action in organizations—instead of simply reacting to events—points us in the right direction.

▨ Reflection

Think of a problem you would like to solve. What is its root cause? To get at the root cause, ask yourself why you have the problem. Then ask why again and again in response to your answer. (Take as much time as you need to do this.) Then ask yourself and others what else might be contributing to this problem. Now ask what about your current systems and structures could be contributing to the problem and what about your own thinking and beliefs play a role? This deeper inquiry will help you get at the underlying causes of the problem. Does your example also illustrate that cause and effect are not closely related in time and space?

Consider what solutions would address the underlying cause and then play out the implementation of these solutions. Who would be affected? How? What would be the costs and benefits across the system? Would implementation inadvertently harm people in other parts of the system?

▨ Notes

_____

_____

_____

_____

_____

DAY 25

Examining Change History

Those who do not remember the past are condemned to repeat it.

—George Santayana

One factor often overlooked in systemic change efforts is an organization's history of change. Change history refers to how the organization has handled changes in the past.

Change history is important for two reasons. First, staff members have recollections of how the organization responded in the past. If change efforts have been successful, the staff will expect new attempts to enjoy success. If the track record shows many failed attempts, then the mindset of the staff will be that the next change will similarly be doomed to failure.

Second, the staff's expectations are likely to be accurate and on target. Success breeds success; past failure suggests future failure unless people believe that something will be different on this occasion.

How do you know what to look for in your organization's change history? Here is a list of questions to ask yourself:

- Did leaders support prior change efforts?

- Were prior change efforts well communicated?

- Did leaders anticipate and plan for the impact of the changes on staff?

- Did the leaders adequately address the needs of individuals?

- Did the leaders commit the resources necessary to implement the change fully?

- Did the leaders model the behaviors they wanted to see in others as the result of the change?

A typical organization pattern is to initiate a major change but fail to provide support for its full implementation. As a result, a change remains only partially implemented, dies out after 2 or 3 years, or is displaced by some other change.

For example, we often hear from people in our Leadership Academy that lack of full support derails their change efforts. A typical scenario: Leaders and staff within a school adopt a new science or mathematics activity-based curriculum, but the supporting structures are never fully provided nor offered over time. Teachers may attend a summer workshop to learn about the new materials, but sustained professional learning isn't forthcoming. Teachers new to the school or grade-changing teachers do not have ongoing opportunities to learn about the curriculum. After a few years, the curriculum is abandoned, and full implementation is never achieved. This pattern can then plague any new initiative.

If this has been the pattern in your organization, then staff and stakeholders are likely to be skeptical of the latest effort. Leaders have to overcome the effects of prior failures and the lingering institutional history to ensure current success. There may be skeptics who won't commit until they see whether this attempt is going to be different. As a leader, you must negotiate for the resources you need in order to implement the changes for which you are responsible.

◈ Reflection

What do you know about your organization's change history? If you don't know about it, how can you find out?

If you know the change history, what does it suggest you need to do to make your current change initiative successful?

◈ Notes

_____

_____

_____

_____

_____

_____

> ### DAY 26
> # The Downside of Change

In order to make things substantially better, you often have to make things worse in the short run.

—Jeffrey Pfeffer

Hmmm, not good news, you say. But it is true. Sometimes the right action that you need to take will make things worse in the short run. That's why leaders will often avoid taking action or they pursue an alternative, although ultimately ineffective, course. Who wants to turn things upside down anyway?

But that's the job of a leader: to see emerging problems and take corrective action to avoid a worsening situation. Not doing so is a failure of leadership, according to the Leader to Leader Institute (2005). Many of such instances are what Bazerman and Watkins (2004) call *predictable surprises*, situations that could be forecasted but are not addressed until they occur. Their classic example is, of course, the terrorist attacks of September 11, 2001. Although not all emerging problems are of such catastrophic magnitude, all organizations have their equivalents. Perhaps it's an impending budget shortfall, plummeting test scores in a school, or rapidly decreasing or increasing participation or enrollment.

There are several reasons why leaders don't respond to a mounting crisis. They may be in denial, hoping the problem will dissipate. Correcting the situation now will be costly, and the long-term benefits are unknown. There is a natural human tendency to resist change and maintain the status quo that affects all humans, including leaders. Also, maintaining the status quo will often benefit some group that will usually lobby on its own behalf (Leader to Leader Institute, 2005).

Bazerman and Watkins (2004) suggest three critical steps for heading off predictable surprises: recognition, prioritization, and mobilization. In *recognition*, leaders take steps to recognize an impending problem earlier. They may do so through studying their past crises or developing scenarios of what might happen in the future, including strategies for addressing problems posed by these various scenarios. In *prioritization*, leaders can participate in structured dialogue. (See Book Four, Days 12 and 13.) An organization may also provide incentives to help leaders reorder their priorities. In *mobilization*, an organization needs to overcome its natural inertia, neutralize opposing factions, and resolve conflicting priorities.

Averting predictable surprises is one of the hardest jobs that a leader has. It requires gathering evidence and rallying people to deal with emerging problems. This is not magical, but it is the hard work of responsible and courageous leaders.

◈ Reflection

Recall at least one example of a predictable surprise that has occurred in your organization. What evidence existed that was ignored? How long was the situation developing? What happened when it became a crisis? What should have been done earlier to avert this crisis?

What crises do you see on your organizational horizon? What is your evidence? What can you do to alert others and take action to avoid another crisis situation?

◈ Notes

_____

_____

_____

_____

_____

_____

_____

_____

DAY 27

Building Ownership for Change

Organizational effectiveness depends upon the sharing or distribution, not the hoarding, of power and influence.

—James M. Kouzes and Barry Z. Posner

"Oh, no. Not *ownership!* I'm so sick of hearing this word. Ownership has become a cliché. Everyone wants me to have ownership. I'm not even sure what the word means anymore."

Have you heard this before? Although ownership has been used somewhat indiscriminately, the basic concept of helping people develop a greater sense of responsibility for and take control of all aspects of their lives is an important leadership characteristic. (See Book One, Day 2.)

Major changes must involve people at all levels of an organization. If people feel no ownership in the change initiative, they are not likely to support or implement it. Instead, they join the group of resisters.

As a leader of a major change initiative, how do you help people develop ownership? You can help them discover what their self-interest is in making the change. How will this change benefit them or their stakeholders? Will their work be easier and more productive? Will the product or service be improved? Will their stakeholders be better off in some way? Once you've clarified self-interest, here are four steps to enable people to develop responsibility and feel more in control of what is happening to them (Kouzes & Posner, 2002):

1. Make sure that they have a sense of power and influence within the organization.

2. Let them know that they have choices, the latitude, and discretion to effectively carry out their tasks.

3. Provide skills and/or attitude training so that they develop competence and confidence.

4. Make sure that they take personal responsibility for themselves and their actions.

Bandura (1997) stresses that leaders should model the skills of building ownership. The three components of effective modeling are leaders exhibiting basic competencies, helping others receive guided practice to perfect their skills, and ensuring opportunities for others to apply their new skills in ways that will help guarantee their success.

◈ Reflection

Consider the people involved in your organization's change effort. On a scale of 1(low) to 10 (high), how much ownership do you think they feel in your initiative? Are there ways you can clarify their self-interest and increase their sense of control, ability to take action, and level of responsibility?

Are you modeling building ownership behaviors? If so, what has been your experience? What would you to do differently?

◈ Notes

_____

_____

_____

_____

_____

_____

_____

_____

DAY 28

Individuals as Agents of Change

I decide. I do. Me.

—Frank Hague

What can a single person do?

So much of Book Two stresses that change is a collaborative effort. It is highly unlikely that a single individual can carry out a major change initiative alone. Organizations are far too complex for one person to exert that degree of influence.

Does that mean there is nothing an individual person can accomplish? Not at all. As a leader, you can serve as a catalyst for change and in that process, serve as a model for others.

At minimum, here is what you can do:

- Commit to being the best you can and pursue a path to high performance.

- Dedicate yourself to being a continual learner and to see problems as opportunities for learning and change.

- Acknowledge your failures and what you have learned.

- Willingly share your knowledge and resources with others who are interested in what you are doing.

- Organize and convene teams to address problems and suggest improvements.

- Offer to coach others.

- Use data for your decision making, and let others know what use you make of this information.

- Articulate your vision, mission, and goals clearly and concisely.

- Actively support change efforts you believe in.

Essentially, you are exhibiting the attitudes and behaviors that are supportive of systemic change. Moreover, you are taking on a leadership role, even though your position may not be one of institutional leadership. If you do these things in a way that is respectful of your colleagues and the organization as a whole, you will make a difference. In fact, you may be the catalyst for starting a major change effort or implementing one.

☒ Reflection

How do you see yourself functioning in your organization? Are you having all the influence that you possibly can? On a scale of 1 (low) to 10 (high), where do you rate yourself on influence? Are there ways you can be more influential?

Of the preceding list, which of the following are you doing now? Which could you do? What would be the likely result?

☒ Notes

_____

_____

_____

_____

_____

_____

_____

_____

DAY 29

Self-Assessment as a Change Leader

Ninety percent of the world's woe comes from people not knowing themselves, their abilities, their frailties, and even their real virtues. Most of us go almost all the way through life as complete strangers to ourselves.

—Sydney J. Harris

Leaders increase their credibility and their likelihood for success if they have experienced what they expect others to do. It is very important for leaders of change to go through major change initiatives themselves. They need to experience resistance firsthand and work through it so they can help others do the same. They need to understand and be committed to personal mastery and exhibit behavior congruent with its principles.

As a leader, you convey what you think and feel more by your actions than by your words. Your colleagues judge you more by what you do than by what you say. Therefore, you need to assess your own personal experience base in dealing with change as part of expanding your leadership role.

◈ Reflection

Here is a list of questions for you to consider as part of your expanding ability to lead change in your organization. It is intended to get you started on your self-assessment.

• Think of two or three changes you have experienced—either personal or professional. What was the impact of the changes on you? Was their impact similar for your colleagues? If the changes had a differential impact, what do you attribute that to?

• When you are experiencing a change, what needs to remain stable in your life? How much change can you handle? How do you know your limit?

• Have you had the experience of grieving for losses when a change has taken place? If so, how have you done that? What works best for you?

• What is your commitment to high performance? Do you have a vision for your work and personal life? Do you view yourself as a continuous learner? Why or why not? Are you committed to stating the truth about your current reality? Can you recall instances in which you have denied the truth about what was currently happening?

• Think of some of your recent leadership decisions or actions. Can you identify what beliefs were influencing you? What assumptions were you making? Did you share these with others so they understood your decision or action better? Are the underlying assumptions you operated with the ones you want? What could you do to change beliefs that no longer work for you?

• How do you use data in your work and life? What are your most reliable sources of information? Are they diverse enough? Can you recall instances in which you ignored data? What were the consequences?

• What is your typical reaction when you discover some problem that you need to address? How might you respond if you regarded a new problem as an opportunity for learning?

• What visions do you have for your professional work? How committed are you to this vision? What would make you more committed to it? Who has a similar vision, or do you hold these visions alone? Is your mission in line with your vision? If not, what do you need to do to make it more so?

• Do you have plans for achieving your visions? What is your plan?

• What is the speed at which you respond to change? How do you assess your speed in relation to the speed of other people? How resilient are you? What would make you more resilient?

Based on your answers to these questions, how comfortable do you feel in leading a major change initiative? What could increase your level of comfort? What kind of experiences are you lacking? How can you get the experience you need?

▧ Notes

DAY 30

Sustaining Individual Leadership

Leaders are the stewards of organizational energy. . . . They inspire or demoralize others first by how effectively they manage their own energy and next by how well they mobilize, focus, invest and renew the collective energy of those they lead.

—Jim Loehr and Tony Schwartz

Recall a time when you felt overwhelmed by all of the changes going on in your organization, your personal life, or both. You probably wanted to call a time out, but there was no slowdown in the flow of events and your need to respond to them.

How does a leader keep going without burning out? Michael Fullan (2005) sees the key to sustaining oneself over time as *cyclical energizing*. This term refers to alternating periods of intense engagement with regular breaks and other energy-regaining methods.

We draw energy from four sources: the physical, emotional, mental, and spiritual (Loehr & Schwartz, 2003). (See Day 13, Motivating Others.) We grow when we stretch ourselves in one or more of these dimensions. If we don't push our limits, we're not likely to expand our capabilities in any of these four areas. However, too much stretch can cause fatigue, burnout, and illness.

The secret to individual sustainability is knowing when and how to conserve and create physical energy, emotional energy, mental energy, and spiritual energy when we need to do so. It's also knowing how to relax and recover after periods of intense challenge and exertion.

Loehr and Schwartz (2003) recommend two specific routines for managing energy. One is the incorporation of rituals into our daily lives; the other, a change of venue, especially one that provides solitude. According to the authors, the power of rituals stems from the fact that they conserve energy. Examples could be morning meditation or a 15-minute walk at lunch time. One of the reasons these rituals are energizing is that we tend to feel worse if we don't do them. "The power of rituals is that they insure that we use as little conscious energy as possible where it is not absolutely necessary, leaving us free to strategically focus the energy available to us in creative, enriching ways" (p. 14).

A great source of personal renewal is going to another venue for a period of time. This is especially valuable when there are opportunities for being alone. An extended period of reflection can lead to heightened self-awareness, greater clarity, more creative thinking, and a stronger sense of self.

◈ Reflection

Choose a recent time period, perhaps the past month; chart the energy demands that you experienced during that time. How would you assess those demands—were they high, medium, or low? If high, how did you respond? How did you feel at the end of the time period? Were you exhausted, or did you find ways to balance your energy intake and expenditure?

What is your normal pattern of "cyclical energizing"? How balanced is it? What can you do to balance your most intense times with downtimes when you can reenergize?

What are the specific ways that you generate physical, emotional, mental, and spiritual energy? Where are you most effective? Where could you improve your skills?

What rituals do you employ to help you conserve energy? How effective are those? Are you able to escape from the crowd and spend time alone? If so, how and how often? How do you assess the value of your time alone?

◈ Notes

_____

_____

_____

_____

_____

_____

_____

_____

DAY 31

Initiating, Implementing, and Institutionalizing Change

Today's successful . . . leaders will be those who are most flexible of mind. An ability to embrace new ideas, routinely challenge old ones, and live with paradox will be the effective leader's premier trait. Further, the challenge is for a lifetime.

—Tom Peters

How do you know if your organization is ready to embark on a major change initiative and be successful over the long haul? Organizations that are prepared to do so have characteristics different from those that are not.

Leaders of organizations that are prepared to launch and sustain major change initiatives do the following:

1. Involve the appropriate stakeholders

2. Think systemically

3. Have a compelling vision that is shared throughout the organization

4. Cultivate a high level of urgency for change

5. Think and act in terms of "both/and" rather than "either/or"

6. Challenge assumptions and mental models

7. Use data for decision making

8. Regularly take time for reflection

9. Consciously manage personal energy

10. Empower people at all levels

11. Create structures with minimal hierarchy, fewer layers, and just the essential rules

12. Regularly conduct environmental scans and/or customer surveys to determine any changes in external influences on the organization

13. Exhibit a high level of risk taking, courage, and avoidance of blame

14. Identify what remains the same and what changes

15. Manage the key elements of change

16. Value continuous improvement

17. Commit the appropriate level of resources to support the change

18. Promote resiliency in people and the organization

19. Designate benchmarks and acknowledge their achievement

20. Celebrate successes and reward progress

21. Have a process for orienting new personnel to the change and securing their support

22. Evaluate the outcomes and plan accordingly

Organizations today don't have the luxury of being able to reject or accept the opportunity to change. They must change, or they will cease to exist. The only open question is how successful they will be with whatever change initiatives they undertake.

☯ Reflection

How does your organization rate on this list? Some single items (Numbers 1, 4, 7, and 17, for example) can instantaneously stall a change initiative if they are not attended to properly.

If your organization is in the midst of a change initiative, how would you rate the effort so far? What has it done well? What needs improvement?

What is the likelihood of your change initiative being institutionalized? If it's low, what needs to happen to increase its chances?

If your organization isn't ready to take on a major change effort but needs to, what can you do to increase the organization's readiness?

☯ Notes

_____

_____

_____

_____

_____

Bibliography

Bandura, A. (1997). *Self-efficacy: The exercise of control.* New York: Freeman.

Barrett, R. (1999). The power of purpose. *Inner Edge, 2*(4), 20–22.

Bazerman, M. H., & Watkins, M. D. (2004). *Predictable surprises: The disasters you should have seen coming and how to prevent them.* Boston: Harvard Business School Press.

Bershad, C., & Mundry, S. (2000). Playing to learn: Systems change game challenges and teaches. *ENC Focus, 7*(1), 24–27.

Block, P. (1991). *The empowered manager: Positive political skills at work.* San Francisco: Jossey-Bass.

Cini, J. (2004). *Kingmaker: Be the one your company wants to keep—on your terms.* Upper Saddle River, NJ: Prentice Hall.

Conner, D. R. (1993). *Managing at the speed of change: How resilient managers succeed and prosper where others fail.* New York: Villard Books.

Conner, D. R. (1998). *Leading at the edge of chaos.* New York: Wiley.

Covey, S. R. (1992*). Principle-based leadership.* London: Simon & Schuster.

Fritz, R. (1989). *The path of least resistance.* New York: Fawcett-Columbine.

Fullan, M. (1993). *Change forces: Probing the depths of educational reform.* London: Falmer.

Fullan, M. (2001). *Leading in a culture of change.* San Francisco: Jossey-Bass.

Fullan, M. (2003). *The moral imperative of school leadership.* Thousand Oaks, CA: Corwin.

Fullan, M. (2005). *Leadership and sustainability: System thinkers in action.* Thousand Oaks, CA: Corwin.

Garmston, R. J., & Wellman, B. M. (1999). *The adaptive school: A sourcebook for developing collaborative groups.* Norwood, MA: Christopher-Gordon.

Hall, G., & Hord, S. (2001). *Implementing change: Patterns, principles, and potholes.* Needham Heights, MA: Allyn & Bacon.

Kaser, J. S., & Horsley, D. (1998a). *Description of a change inventory process.* Albuquerque, NM: Kaser and Associates.

Kaser, J. S., & Horsley, D. (1998b). *Sources of resistance.* Albuquerque, NM: Kaser and Associates.

Kotter, J. P. (1996). *Leading change.* Boston: Harvard Business School Press.

Kouzes, J. M., & Posner, B. Z. (2002). *The leadership challenge.* San Francisco: Jossey-Bass.

Kübler-Ross, E. (1970). *On death and dying.* New York: Macmillan.

Leader to Leader Institute. (2004, Summer). From the front lines: Practical wisdom: Dealing effectively with disappointment. *Leader to Leader, 33,* 60–61.

Leader to Leader Institute. (2005, Winter). From the front lines: Executive challenges: Tough talk about leadership failure. *Leader to Leader, 35,* 53–54.

Loehr, J., & Schwartz, T. (2003). *The power of full engagement.* New York: Free Press.

Loucks-Horsley, S., & Stiegelbauer, S. (1991). Using knowledge of change to guide staff development. In A. Lieberman & L. Miller (Eds.), *Staff development for education in the '90s: New demands, new realities, new perspectives* (pp. 15–36). New York: Teachers College Press.

Mundry, S., & Bershad, C. (1998). *Systems thinking/systems changing: A simulation game.* Andover, MA: The NETWORK. (cbers@comcast.net)

Senge, P. M. (1990). *The fifth discipline.* New York: Doubleday.

Senge, P. M., Kleiner, A., Roberts, C., Ross, R. B., Roth, G., & Smith, B. J. (1999). *The dance of change.* New York: Doubleday.

Senge, P. M., Kleiner, A., Roberts, C., Ross, R. B., & Smith, B. J. (1994). *The fifth discipline fieldbook: Strategies and tools for building a learning organization.* New York: Doubleday.

Vaill, P. B. (1992). *Managing as a performing art.* New York: Villard Books.

Book Three

▨ Leading Learning Communities

B ook Three is a collection of thoughts and inspirations on leading learning within increasingly diverse communities. The leader's role is to carefully design and nurture the conditions that promote learning for all—individuals, teams, and organizations. The 31 contemplations herein provide information to help leaders promote learning for themselves and the individuals with whom they work.

Leading learning communities requires knowledge of current research and best practice on learning communities, the roles of leaders within those communities, how adults learn and under what conditions, and how to create and sustain environments that focus on continuous learning and improvement. In the first contemplations we engage leaders in thinking about several questions: What is a learning community? How do individuals within these communities best learn? What constitutes powerful learning? What do we know about how adults learn? How do adults transfer learning from one context to another? Why is developing expertise within a community valuable?

With Day 11 we focus on what we know from research and best practice about the process of designing professional development experiences and programs for adult learners. Some of the questions explored include: How do we design professional development programs that align our beliefs and assumptions with our behaviors and actions? What roles do vision and a commitment to standards play in designing professional development? How can we best use data to assess our needs and guide our designs?

We prompt leaders to address questions such as: How do we create balanced programs? How do we sustain adult learning programs? What should we consider when expanding programs? How do we know if our anticipated outcomes have been achieved?

Days 30 and 31 ask leaders to explore the ways in which they lead learning by example and what steps they can take to become more effective leaders of learning communities.

The questions in Book Three are grouped around four themes that are interwoven throughout the 31 contemplations:

1. What are the characteristics of learning communities? What are culturally proficient communities? What role do leaders play in developing learning communities?

2. What do we know from research about how people learn? What are the contexts that support effective learning?

3. What is effective professional development? What are the inputs into designing professional development? How do we evaluate program effectiveness?

4. What are the strategies for professional development? How do we align strategies with outcomes and results?

DAY 1
Leading Communities of Learning

Leadership and learning are indispensable to each other.
—John F. Kennedy

Communities of learning, professional learning communities, communities of practice, self-renewing organizations, learning organizations—what do these phrases convey about organizations and the people within them?

Clearly, *learning* is at the core of each one. The implication is that not only do the individuals within the organization have opportunities to learn, but also that the organizations learn. For example, given that we live in a world where new knowledge is continuously discovered and one that is constantly changing, it follows that organizations, and the people within them, cannot remain static. In order to adapt and evolve, organizations need structures and processes for obtaining, sharing, and learning from the information that most directly impacts them and their clients. As Michael Fullan (2001) writes, "Leaders commit themselves to constantly generating and increasing knowledge inside and outside the organization" (p. 6) and "make knowledge building a core value" (p. 90). To support and enact their commitments they initiate and sustain ways in which to engage people in generating and sharing knowledge. (See Book One, Day 10.)

With knowledge and learning at the core of an organization's values, there is a parallel need for collegial and collaborative processes to enable people to engage in learning together and to share what they have learned from external sources. Nowhere is this more critical than in schools. Richard DuFour and others (DuFour, DuFour, Eaker, & Karhanek, 2004) write about "professional learning communities" (PLCs) and state that there are six key characteristics that distinguish PLCs from more traditional schools (see Book One, Day 17). In combination, these six characteristics can provide the organizational values and structures for becoming a learning community:

1. Shared mission, vision, values, and goals

2. Collaborative teams

3. Collective inquiry

4. Action orientation and experimentation

5. Continuous improvement

6. Results orientation

Combining Fullan's concept of "knowledge creation and sharing" with DuFour's "professional learning communities" provides leaders with a framework for rethinking the concept of organizations and schools as static places to work. Learning in and of itself becomes a product of an organization and, in the process, builds a culture that values and embodies continuous learning, growth, and change. Leaders need to create the motivation and commitment to learn among people in their organizations and create the environment—time, structures, and incentives—for learning to happen.

▨ Reflection

Think about an organization you have been involved with that did not have a commitment to learning. What happened to this organization? How did this organization ignore or disregard new information or knowledge that could have greatly enhanced its effectiveness? What structures were missing that could have provided knowledge generation and sharing among individuals?

Now, recall the opposite situation—a situation where you were encouraged to learn continuously and the organization valued new knowledge as a source of information for adapting and changing. How did the organization manifest its commitment? How did you and your colleagues feel? What difference did this make in the organization? In what ways did the organization change as a result of new information or knowledge? What characteristics of a community of learners did this organization have?

What about the organization you are part of now? To what extent do your colleagues see learning as a value and an explicit goal of the organization? What can you do to promote a community of learning and knowledge generation and sharing? Do you personally value, model, and contribute to a community of learners?

❧ Notes

DAY 2
Individuals in Learning Communities

Experience is not what happens to you; it's what you do with what happens to you.

—Aldous Huxley

Knowledge of what contributes to effective individual learning must drive the structures and processes that leaders establish within their organizations and learning communities. That knowledge is drawn from research and best practice (for example, Bransford, Brown, & Cocking, 1999, and Donovan & Bransford, 2005; Owen, Cox, & Watkins, 1994) and is reflected in Owen et al.'s (1994) 12 principles of knowledge acquisition:

1. People are born learners. Notice the natural curiosity of children. All humans are born with an intrinsic motivation to learn.

2. People seek to understand new information and experiences by connecting them to what they already know. New knowledge must be connected to prior knowledge for effective learning to occur.

3. People learn in different ways. Research has documented the fact that people have inclinations toward learning through particular styles or approaches.

4. Thinking about one's own thinking improves performance and the ability to work independently. The ability to stand back and observe one's own thought process is an important skill of effective learners.

5. An individual's stage of intellectual, social, and emotional development affects how he or she learns.

6. Although people may naturally make connections as they learn, they often need help to transfer knowledge or apply it in different contexts. Unconnected knowledge is rarely retained.

7. Having a repertoire of strategies enhances learning. Learning is essentially a process of problem solving. The greater the variety of strategies for achieving a goal that a learner has, the more successful he or she is likely to be.

8. Certain predispositions, attitudes, and habits of mind facilitate learning. Qualities such as flexibility, open-mindedness, reflection, and empathy promote learning. Rigidity, bias, tunnel vision, and impulsiveness are barriers to learning.

9. Working with people who have different learning styles and perspectives enhances learning. Working in a diverse group can stimulate members to engage in higher-order cognitive skills.

10. Those who do the work do the learning. Effective learners create knowledge for themselves, own it, know why they learned it, and how they learned it.

11. A resource-rich environment facilitates learning. For learners to actively construct knowledge, they need access to a wide variety of materials. These include ideas, books, visual and auditory media, technology, artifacts, and opportunities to interact.

12. Developing shared understandings about what constitutes quality work fosters learning. Effective learners integrate their internal goals with external expectations. (Owen et al., 1994, pp. 16–29)

These 12 principles, in addition to what we know about how people learn as described in Days 5 through 9, provide leaders with a wealth of information to build on in creating communities of individual learners.

◈ Reflection

Reread each of the 12 principles. As you do so, think about how you have experienced each of these in your life.

Review the principles a second time to look at how each applies to how your organization supports individual learning. Are certain principles reflected in your organization? How are they reflected? Are certain principles not being honored? If so, what can you do to make sure all these principles are incorporated into your organization's culture?

◈ Notes

_____

_____

_____

_____

_____

_____

_____

_____

_____

_____

_____

DAY 3

Building Cultural Proficiency

In the end, we will remember not the words of our enemies, but the silence of our friends.

—Martin Luther King Jr.

As leaders, we have a moral responsibility to increase our own and our learning community's cultural proficiency by engaging others in conversations about equity, diversity, and culture.

We work within multicultural organizations and schools; and as facilitators and leaders of communities of learners, we often face the challenge of engaging our colleagues in dialogue about race, diversity, and culture. People may fail to see the diversity that exists among the different people they work with or how it is going to increase as our population diversifies. Or they may mistakenly believe that being blind to color, race, gender, or disability is desirable.

What Is Cultural Proficiency?

According to Lindsey, Robins, and Terrell (2003), "Cultural proficiency is a way of being that enables both individuals and organizations to respond effectively to people who differ from them" (p. 5). Lindsey and his colleagues (Lindsey, Robins, & Terrell, 2003; Lindsey, Roberts, & CampbellJones, 2005) describe a continuum that reflects individuals' and organizations' "healthy and destructive" behaviors, including:

Cultural Proficiency Continuum

• *Cultural destructiveness:* The elimination of other people's cultures by negating, disparaging, or purging cultures that are different from your own. "See the difference, stomp it out."

• *Cultural incapacity:* Believing in the superiority of one's culture and cultural values and engaging in behaviors that disempower or suppress cultures that are different from your own. "See the difference, make it wrong."

• *Cultural blindness:* Acting as if the cultural differences you see do not matter or do not exist, or not recognizing that there are differences among and between cultures. "See the difference, act like you don't."

- *Cultural precompetence:* Recognizing that the lack of knowledge, experience, and understanding of other cultures limits your ability to effectively interact with them. "See the difference, respond inadequately."

- *Cultural competence:* Interacting with other cultural groups in ways that recognize and value their differences, motivate you to assess your own skills, expand your knowledge and resources, and, ultimately, cause you to adapt your relational behavior. "See the difference, understand the difference that *difference* makes."

- *Cultural proficiency:* Honoring the differences among cultures, seeing diversity as a benefit, interacting knowledgeably and respectfully among a variety of cultural groups, and knowing how to learn about individual and organizational culture. "See the differences, respond positively and affirmingly."

As leaders, being aware of the continuum and raising others' awareness of and dialogue about the continuum is a first step toward reaching cultural proficiency.

▧ Reflection

Think about each level of the cultural proficiency continuum. Where do you believe that you personally lie on the continuum? What behaviors do you engage in that support your perception? Where do you believe the people in your organization or school lie on the continuum? What collective behaviors or practices do people in the organization engage in that support your perception?

Think about a recent experience in which another person's values reflected either cultural destructiveness, incapacity, or blindness. How did you respond? Does your awareness of the continuum change the way you might respond to this person in the future? As a leader, what responsibility do you believe you have to confront and challenge others' destructive behaviors concerning cultures different than their own?

◈ Notes

DAY 4

Powerful Learning Experiences

Epiphany—any sudden and important manifestation or realization.

—Oxford English Dictionary

Whether we call it an "aha!" experience or the moment when "the light goes on," we have all had powerful learning experiences. These experiences often occur when we connect new information to something we already know and understand, and it takes us farther in our thinking.

An analysis of our "light bulb" experiences can give us insight into how we learn best, what learning is most important to us, and the circumstances in which the learning occurs (Owen et al., 1994). Let's see whether this is the case for you.

🔷 Reflection

Think about a learning experience in your life that had a powerful impact. It could have been an event from your formal schooling or any aspect of your life. It could be something that happened recently or a long time ago. You may recall it as being either pleasant or unpleasant.

First, recreate this experience in your mind. Imagine being in the situation again. What happened? What did you do? What were you feeling? What did others do? What was the impact? Did the influence of this experience occur immediately or later?

After you have a clear picture of the event, write a brief description of it.

Now, answer the following questions about your powerful learning experience:

• Where did your experience occur?

• What were the characteristics of the learning? Think in terms of the connections, the conditions, the environment, and resources available.

• Was there a teacher of some sort present? If so, what role did this person play? What role did you play in this experience?

• If your experience was positive, what would be necessary for it to be duplicated either within or outside of formal schooling?

• If your experience was negative, is this something that should be avoided? If so, what would be necessary to make sure that others did not have this same experience?

In our Leadership Academy, we have facilitated this activity with hundreds of leaders from diverse contexts and settings. In each case, only about 25 percent of the people report that their most powerful learning experiences were school related. Most are informal learning experiences, such as continuing education courses, museum programs, or church activities. Others are learning from their day-to-day interactions. What do you think this suggests about designing adult learning experiences in your organization?

Relate your powerful learning experience to any efforts that you are currently implementing to build a community of learners within your organization. How have your colleagues or clients been affected? As a leader, how can you make sure that others have powerful learning experiences?

◈ Notes

_____

_____

_____

_____

_____

_____

_____

_____

DAY 5

How People Learn

Learning is not attained by chance, it must be sought for with ardor and attended to with diligence.

—Abigail Adams

Knowledge of how people learn is a critical input into the design and implementation of adult learning experiences. Think for a moment about how you learn new information. What do you know about how others learn?

From recent research (Bransford et al., 1999; Donovan & Bransford, 2005), we continue to add to our knowledge base on the ways in which adults and students learn. This knowledge of how people learn can be instrumental in designing both student and adult learning opportunities and includes the concepts that:

- New knowledge is built on the learner's prior knowledge.

- Learning is an active process.

- Knowledge is constructed through a process of change.

- New knowledge comes from experiences and interaction with ideas and phenomena.

- Learning needs to be situated in meaningful and relevant contexts.

- Learning is supported through interaction among learners about the concepts and ideas of the new knowledge.

Opportunities for learning that embody the research on how people learn pay attention to creating four types of learning environments (Bransford et al., 1999; Donovan & Bransford, 2005):

1. *Learner-centered environments* encourage attention to preconceptions and initiate learning based on what people currently think and know.

2. *Knowledge-centered environments* focus on what is to be learned, why it is important to learn it, and what mastery of the knowledge looks like.

3. *Assessment-centered environments* emphasize frequent and ongoing assessment of what the learner knows and thinks in order to guide and inform instructional next steps.

4. *Community-centered environments* foster a culture of questioning, respect, risk taking, and interactive engagement.

◈ Reflection

Think about your own school and ask yourself the following questions:

• To what extent do the adult and student learning activities you are involved in reflect the research on how people learn? What areas need more emphasis?

• In what ways do you as a leader promote and provide opportunities that value the ways that people learn?

• Would your school's approach to learning be characterized by any one of the four learning environments? Since all four environments are critical, what could you do to enhance any that are not currently embedded in the structures of your school?

• As a leader, what could you do to enhance your colleagues' awareness of the research on how people learn and the environments that support that learning?

◈ Notes

_____

_____

_____

_____

_____

_____

DAY 6

Transformative Learning

We cannot solve problems with the same thinking that created them.

—Albert Einstein

What implications does the knowledge base on how people learn have for the ways in which leaders design and implement adult learning experiences?

One implication is that adult learning experiences must transform current thinking and practices rather than simply adding new skills and ideas on top of the old. In additive learning, the goal is to acquire new skills and incorporate them into an existing repertoire. The goal of transformative learning is to change deeply held beliefs, knowledge, and habits of practice. Additive learning alone will not suffice when new ways of thinking about something are also needed (Thompson & Zeuli, 1999).

Thompson and Zeuli (1999) describe five distinguishing characteristics of transformative learning:

1. It creates cognitive dissonance, a disruption in someone's thinking, causing them to struggle to make sense of something that doesn't fit with their current ideas.

2. It provides time, contexts, and support for adults to resolve this dissonance by engaging over time with facilitators who have had experience in coaching and mentoring.

3. It ensures that the dissonance-creating and dissonance-resolving activities are relevant to the participant.

4. It provides a means for adults to develop new practices that are congruent with the new ideas they are constructing.

5. It ensures adults of continuing help in the cycle of surfacing the new issues and problems they will encounter, gaining new understandings from these experiences, translating new understandings from them, and recycling through the process.

Transformative learning requires designing experiences that challenge participants' current thinking and often startle them into new beliefs (cognitive dissonance). The old way can be described as evolutionary tinkering within the traditional paradigm. This contrasts sharply with revolutionary changes that transform the basic thinking and beliefs of participants.

In education, cognitive dissonance can occur when teachers engage with student thinking and assess how well their current methods address the students' learning. Teachers are likely to discover that using the same old approaches to teach more challenging content just is not effective. They see the need to rethink what they do and how they interact with students. These experiences produce discomfort with current practice and the need to adapt to create better outcomes.

Both additive and transformative adult learning experiences may be necessary. Additive learning is appropriate for developing new skills. However, learners must understand the assumptions and beliefs that guide the skill; or they may learn the skill well but lack the understanding of why they are using it. Transformative learning focuses more on making shifts in assumptions and beliefs and helping learners understand why a new approach might be necessary. The emphasis of education today is moving toward integrating both transformative and additive learning.

▨ Reflection

Think of a learning experience that created cognitive dissonance for you. What were you thinking and feeling? How did you resolve it? We often resolve dissonance by rejecting the new idea and holding fast to our prior beliefs. Without challenge and support to get to the other side of the dissonance, learning will not occur.

Think about the adult learning that has transpired in your school. Would you describe it as more additive or transformative, or as both? Give some examples to support your answer. If you think that your school needs adult learning experiences that are more transformative, what can you as a leader do to help make that happen? If you think both additive and transformative learning are needed, how might you integrate them?

▨ Notes

DAY 7

Transferring Situational Learning

Learning is important because no one is born with the ability to function competently as an adult in society.

—John Bransford, Ann Brown, and Rodney Cocking

Ideally, the learning experiences we engage in apply to real-life situations and help us to be productive workers, responsible citizens, competent parents, and have rewarding relationships. However, even if we are provided with transformative learning opportunities, not all our learning experiences ensure that we will successfully transfer the knowledge to new situations or contexts.

What promotes knowledge transfer? What impedes it? Research (Bransford et al., 1999) shows the following:

• Knowledge and skills must be beyond the narrow context in which they are first learned. As an example, knowing how to solve a mathematics problem in school doesn't automatically mean that one can solve similar problems in real life.

• Learners must understand when it is appropriate to apply what they have learned. The conditions of applicability must be made clear; it cannot be assumed that the learner will necessarily see the connection.

• To be widely applicable or transferable, learning must be based on generalized principles. For example, what is learned by rote memory can rarely be transferred. On the other hand, understanding general principles, which can be applied to a variety of situations, promotes transfer.

• Transfer is more likely to occur if learners have conceptual rather than just factual knowledge. For example, conceptual knowledge includes an understanding of part-whole relationships and similarities and differences.

• Individuals who see themselves as both learners and thinkers are better at transfer. They are better able to monitor their own level of understanding and its application.

• Learners need to have sufficient time on task to adequately process information. Learning can't be rushed if the ability to transfer is to develop.

• Prior experiences can help or hinder new learning and, as a result, transfer. Some "unlearning" of misconceptions may have to take place or adjustments made to accommodate new knowledge.

❖ Reflection

Recall one or two adult learning experiences that you have designed or facilitated. To what extent did they result in the ability to transfer learning into other contexts and real-world examples? What was designed into them to ensure that such transfer would occur? What evidence do you have that transfer took place?

❖ Notes

_____

_____

_____

_____

_____

_____

_____

_____

_____

> ## DAY 8
> # Defining Expertise

I wish we could understand the word expert as expressing an attitude of mind which we can all acquire rather than the collecting of information by a special caste.

—Mary Parker Follett

Learning communities not only value continuous learning, but also the development and nurturing of expertise within the system. Effective leaders have expertise, and truly collaborative communities have experts at all levels of the system. In fact, a goal within learning communities, especially schools, should be to develop expertise among all members (Stiles & Mundry, 2002).

What is an *expert?* Why is it important to develop everyone's expertise? Is *expert* a general term used to describe someone who knows a lot about a specific subject? Exactly what makes someone an expert? Is there a line that one crosses to move into expertise?

Interestingly, recent research has revealed clear distinctions between novices and experts. Expertise is not just the possession of general abilities, such as memory or intelligence, nor is it the use of general strategies. Instead, experts have extensive knowledge that affects their perceptions and how they process information. This affects what they remember, how they reason, and how they solve problems—all very important attributes of leaders and of every member within a learning community.

Recent research shows the following:

- Experts notice features and meaningful patterns of information that novices don't detect.

- Experts have acquired a great deal of content knowledge that is highly organized. Their organization of information reflects a deep understanding of the subject matter.

- Experts' knowledge cannot be reduced to sets of isolated facts or propositions, but instead, reflects contexts of applicability—it is conditionalized.

- Experts are able to retrieve important aspects of their knowledge with little effort.

• Though experts know their disciplines thoroughly, this does not guarantee that they are able to instruct others about the topic.

• Experts have varying levels of flexibility in their approaches to new situations. (Bransford et al., 1999, p. xiii)

What are some of the implications of these findings for adult learning within schools and other educational settings?

All learners—both students and teachers—can profit from practice with identifying patterns, understanding problems in terms of underlying concepts or big ideas, using models of how experts approach and solve problems, recognizing relevant versus irrelevant information, determining conditions under which information is important, and being able to retrieve the right information with ease. Teachers who develop these skills as experts also consciously incorporate learning experiences for their students that provide opportunities to develop students as experts.

School-based adult learning programs need to more frequently embed what we know about developing experts into their programs. As Stiles and Mundry (2002) write:

> If school-based professional development programs are to gain a return on their professional development investment in terms of student learning, educators must transform their programs for professional learning, provide professional development that reflects how people learn, and build teacher expertise over time. Building teacher expertise should become the very purpose of professional learning in schools. (p. 140)

◈ Reflection

Do you consider yourself an expert in one or more areas? If so, to what extent do these research findings apply to you? Do you see yourself as needing additional knowledge and/or skills to become an expert?

If you want to grow in your expertise, what steps can you take?

Does your organization or school recognize the value of experts and encourage the development of expertise? As a leader, what can you do to help others develop expertise?

◈ Notes

_____

_____

_____

_____

_____

_____

_____

_____

_____

_____

_____

_____

_____

DAY 9

Characteristics of Effective Professional Learning

In most schools, a large gap exists between what is known about professional learning that affects teaching and improves student achievement and the professional development that teachers and principals regularly experience. The solution to [this] problem, I believe, is high-quality, school-based professional learning and collaborative work that affects all teachers virtually every day.

—Dennis Sparks

What did professional learning in education used to look like? How is it changing?

Historically, in the field of education, most adult learning was provided through in-service workshops. Rarely did teachers have a voice in the types of learning opportunities that would best meet their emerging needs. Too often, these workshops did little to help teachers connect new learning with their own teaching practices or provide follow-up experiences to deepen and extend learning and practice.

Today, professional learning in schools is moving in a different direction. Due to the changing emphasis in schools to become communities of learning and practice, teachers and other educators have opportunities to engage in new learning that is directly related to their learning needs and those of their students. This new emphasis on practice-based professional learning has several distinguishing characteristics, such as:

- Directly relating the learning opportunities to the school's goals and the teachers' needs in meeting those goals

- Supporting teachers in making explicit connections between what they do and what their students learn

- Building a learning community in which all take responsibility for learning and working collegially to share knowledge, insight, and experience

- Empowering teachers to design, conduct, and follow through on their own learning, with multiple learning experiences provided over time and with greater depth

- Promoting practice, reflection, and refinement in a safe environment in which teachers can take risks and explore new practices

- Requiring accountability for learning and outcomes

- Continuously monitoring and evaluating the successes and challenges within the context

These characteristics are based on what we know about the principles of effective adult learning designs (Loucks-Horsley, Love, Stiles, Mundry, & Hewson, 2003). The knowledge base and common vision that has developed in the past several years is that effective professional development:

- Is driven by an image of effective classroom learning and teaching

- Is designed to address student learning needs identified through data analysis

- Provides opportunities for teachers to build their content and pedagogical content knowledge and critically examine practice

- Is research based and engages teachers in learning approaches they will use with their students

- Provides opportunities for teachers to collaborate with colleagues and other experts

- Supports teachers to serve in leadership roles

- Provides links to other parts of the educational system

- Is continuously evaluated and improved

◈ Reflection

If you have been with your school or district for some time, write a list of about a dozen words that describe the professional learning opportunities as practiced 8 to 10 years ago. Then, generate a list of about a dozen words that describe your more recent learning opportunities. What differences do you see? What accounts for these differences? If you don't see changes, why not? Is your focus on professional learning stuck, or is it evolving? If it is stuck, what can you do to get it out of the mire?

In what ways does your current adult learning program reflect what we know about effective professional development? Which principles does your program embody? Which ones are missing? In what ways would you like to enhance your program?

◈ Notes

DAY 10

Aligning Assumptions and Behaviors

The thing always happens that you really believe in; and the belief in a thing makes it happen.

—Frank Lloyd Wright

Alignment is one of the key words used in educational change. For example, we talk about curriculum and professional development being aligned with local and state standards. Likewise, we encourage organizations to align structures with their visions and missions.

Another area of alignment is ensuring the congruency between what we believe and how we behave. It means identifying our underlying assumptions about teaching and learning and determining whether our behavior is consistent with our beliefs. For example, if leaders believe that the ideas reflected in Days 4 through 9 are critical for adult learning, do they indeed act upon those beliefs? When you examine what is going on in schools today, several inconsistencies stand out (see Table 3.1).

These inconsistencies may have several different causes:

- Not examining the underlying assumptions and not recognizing the discrepancies in behavior

- Not seeing the lack of alignment as a problem that needs to be addressed

- Changes in organizational culture normally lag behind other types of institutional changes; adopting a new curriculum is much easier than getting everyone to become proficient in teaching it

- Existing resources are insufficient to support the change effort

◈ Reflection

Examining individual and organizational beliefs and assumptions is a critical first step for ensuring that we provide effective and powerful adult learning opportunities. Think about your own organization. Generate a list of "what we say" beliefs and then the corresponding "what we do" actions. What incongruities exist in your own context? What other incongruities not listed in Table 3.1 can you identify? What are the causes for these discrepancies?

Table 3.1   Examples of Misalignment

What We Say	*What We Do*
Teacher learning is the centerpiece of effective change.	Provide a few hours of in-service each year.
Students should be independent, self-directed learners.	Give teachers little say regarding the content or process of their own professional development.
Teaching is a complex process of decision making requiring a wide range of instructional strategies to meet individual learner needs.	Limit the instructional strategies teachers experience in professional development to courses and workshops.
Every child, every teacher, and every organization is in some ways unique, and programs need to be tailored to meet individual needs.	Reduce professional development to "one size fits all."
Change is long term.	Direct professional development resources to "one-shot" workshops without follow-up support.
Change is systemwide.	Work with volunteers, the early adopters, which produces pockets of change rather than systemwide change.

How can you engage your colleagues in looking for and surfacing misalignments and inconsistencies?

⬙ Notes

_____

_____

_____

_____

_____

DAY 11

Designing Professional Development

A bridge, like professional development, is a critical link between where one is and where one wants to be. A bridge that works in one place almost never works in another. Each bridge requires careful design that considers its purpose, who will use it, the conditions that exist at its anchor points . . . and the resources required to construct it. Similarly, each professional development program . . . requires a careful and unique design.

—Susan Loucks-Horsley

The key ideas raised in many of the previous days' contemplations reinforce the need for leaders to design and implement adult learning experiences that build on beliefs, assumptions, and knowledge. However, knowing what we believe and acting in accordance with those beliefs is not the only important step. Leaders also need to thoroughly understand their context, the learning needs and goals of the people within that context, the issues that may be critical for success, and how to evaluate whether specific outcomes have been achieved.

As the quotation points out, each context is different. There is no one right way to approach the design and implementation of professional development; each bridge is unique. There are, however, frameworks for designing learning experiences based on what we know to be effective.

Leaders of learning are often in the position of designing, or suggesting that others design, professional development activities for individuals or groups. Effective professional development addresses a number of important and fairly specific issues or factors. It isn't cobbled together; it isn't cookie cutter; it isn't the innovation du jour. It is consciously and deliberately designed.

Figure 3.1 presents one framework for designing professional development for both individual and group learning (Loucks-Horsley et al., 2003).

The framework reflects an implementation process that serves as the foundation for effective adult learning programs, and includes:

- A commitment to vision and the standards

- An analysis of student learning needs and other schoolwide data

Figure 3.1 Design Framework for Professional Development in Science and Mathematics

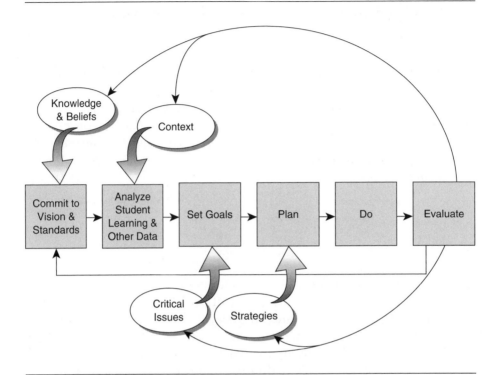

SOURCE: Loucks-Horsley, Love, Stiles, Mundry, and Hewson, Copyright 2003. *Designing Professional Development for Teachers of Science and Mathematics, second edition* (p. 4). Thousand Oaks, CA: Corwin. Reprinted with permission.

- A set of clearly defined goals and intended outcomes
- A plan that includes a combination of professional development strategies aligned with the goals and outcomes
- An articulated and sequential design for taking action
- A process for gathering data, reflecting on learning, evaluating effectiveness, and making adjustments based on that information

◈ Reflection

Think about a professional development program that you have been a part of and answer the following questions:

- What was the vision that drove the need for and design of the program?

- What student learning or adult learning needs were identified prior to the design of the program?

- What were the goals and desired outcomes?

- Were the strategies aligned to meet those goals and outcomes?

- How did you know if the goals and outcomes had been met?

- What changes in the program did you make based on continuous learning and evaluation?

If you had been in charge of this professional development program, what would you have done differently?

❧ Notes

_____

_____

_____

_____

_____

_____

_____

_____

DAY 12

Committing to Vision and Standards

The description of the national standards was clear enough that they could recognize the difference between what the standards said should be happening and what currently was going on in their own school.

—Harold Pratt

What is your school's or organization's vision? To what extent is that vision an extension of the standards that guide your work?

In education, educators rely on national and local standards to guide almost every aspect of schooling, from adopting curriculum and selecting instructional materials to guiding best practice in the classroom. These documents serve as both a banner for reform and a template for guiding decisions about policies and practices (for example, American Association for the Advancement of Science, 1993; National Council of Teachers of Mathematics, 1989, 1991, 1995, 2000; National Research Council, 1996). In addition, the professional development standards (National Staff Development Council, 2001) articulate a vision of what we need to know and do in professional development to provide all educators with high quality and effective adult learning experiences.

Included in the national standards are images and vignettes of effective science and mathematics teaching and learning that schools can use to define and refine their own vision. Contemplations that appear in Books One and Two describe the importance of leaders developing, building, and sustaining vision. In designing professional development, leaders need to facilitate dialogue among teachers, administrators, parents, community members, and other stakeholders to ensure a common vision of who and what the school wants to become. The emerging professional development design should be firmly grounded in this vision of what we know about teaching and learning and effective professional development.

◈ Reflection

What is your vision for teaching and learning? How was that vision developed? What do teachers need to know and be able to do to create classrooms that align with this vision?

As a leader, what role have you played in developing this common vision? To what extent is that vision based on the national and local standards?

◈ Notes

_____

_____

_____

_____

_____

_____

_____

_____

_____

_____

DAY 13

Using Data to Guide
Professional Development Design

In a rush to "do" something, schools may latch onto popular or simplistic solutions to resolve complex problems. Data help school staff dig deeper, consider the local context, and more fully understand a problem before jumping into action.

—Nancy Love

How close is your current reality to your vision? How do you know?

Gathering and analyzing schoolwide data can provide you with the information necessary to determine where you are in relationship to the vision you have developed. Leaders can then guide the development of an effective program that ensures they are addressing the critical areas in need of improvement.

Today's schools are inundated with data and are constantly given the message that data-driven decision making is essential for meeting accountability standards. Often, the data that schools have access to are not the most relevant for understanding individual student's and teacher's knowledge or skills. It is exactly this type of data that is needed to guide the design of a professional development program that meets all learners' needs.

The data that are most relevant for informing professional development programs consist of:

- Demographic data about students and teachers

- Multiple measures of students' achievement of standards

- Student learning data disaggregated by racial, economic, language, and gender groups

- Data about classroom practice and students' opportunity to learn

- Data about professional development, the school culture, and leadership (Loucks-Horsley et al., 2003, p. 18)

These data provide valuable information about your current context, student learning needs, equitable practices, teacher learning needs, and classroom practices. In combination, these data provide the baseline information that drives the specific design of an effective professional development program that moves a school closer to meeting the vision.

◈ Reflection

Think about the data you have access to and the ways in which you use those data to guide schoolwide improvement efforts. In what ways do you use data to determine existing student learning needs? How have you used data to identify what teachers need to know and be able to do in order to meet student learning needs? To what extent is examining data a regular, schoolwide, and collaborative effort? What data do you not have that would better inform your design for schoolwide improvement? How could you obtain such data?

◈ Notes

_____

_____

_____

_____

_____

_____

_____

_____

DAY 14

Inputs Into Professional Development Design

Many locally developed programs have been enormously successful in improving student achievement. However, successful replication across sites suggests that a program's accomplishments are less dependent on the characteristics of an individual school and more related to the design of the staff development effort.

—Joellen Killion

Designers of adult learning opportunities must consider four important inputs into the design process. (See Figure 3.1.)

1. *Knowledge and beliefs:* The design must reflect the knowledge base on learning, teaching, the nature of the subject matter, professional development, the change process, and the fundamental beliefs that will guide you.

2. *Context:* The design must suit the context in which the learning will take place and the teaching will occur. The context includes learners, teachers, practices (for example, curriculum, instruction, and assessment), the learning environment, policies, resources, organizational culture, organizational structure, history of professional development, and stakeholders, such as parents and community members.

3. *Critical issues:* The design must take into account those elements that will affect—either positively or negatively—the success of the overall program. Examples include ensuring equity, finding time for professional development, building professional culture, developing leadership, building capacity for sustainability, scaling up, and garnering support.

4. *Strategies:* The design must reflect the different approaches to learning that are most appropriate given the purposes and context. Examples include strategies within six categories: aligning and implementing curriculum, collaborative structures, examining teaching and learning, immersion experiences, practicing teaching, and vehicles and mechanisms. (Loucks-Horsley et al., 2003)

These inputs, in combination with the design process, create a dynamic whole that must be considered as you design professional development. The factors all influence and contribute to each other, are iterative and cyclical, and continuously change, so one must stay tuned to the environment to adapt to these changing circumstances.

◈ Reflection

Think about a professional development program that you have been a part of and answer the following questions:

• What assumptions did the learning program make about the nature of teaching, learning, the content, and the change process? How were they guided by research?

• Did the learning program take the context of the school or district into account? If so, how?

• What strategies of teaching and learning did the program employ? Were they the right ones for the situation? Would you have chosen different strategies? If so, describe what and why.

• How successful was the learning program? How do you know? Were there any critical issues that the program did or didn't address that affected the outcome?

◈ Notes

_____

_____

_____

_____

_____

DAY 15

Knowledge and Beliefs

Knowledge is of two kinds. We know a subject ourselves, or we know where we can find information on it.

—Samuel Johnson

What are the beliefs and knowledge that guide leaders' designs of effective professional development programs?

Knowledge refers to information that is supported by and grounded in research. *Beliefs* are what we think we know (Ball, 1996) based on our current information. Beliefs also inform our perspective on and interpretation of new knowledge—beliefs serve as our personal filters for how we deal with new knowledge.

According to Loucks-Horsley and colleagues (2003), five distinct, but related, knowledge bases inform the work of professional developers and include what we know about:

1. Effective professional development

2. Learners and learning

3. Teachers and teaching

4. Change and the change process

5. Nature of the disciplines or content areas

The first four knowledge bases are discussed in contemplations throughout Books One, Two, and Three. The fifth knowledge base is discussed here.

Nature of the Disciplines

Every discipline or content area has its own set of standards or frameworks that guide what we should know and be able to do to become literate adults. However, some disciplines, specifically science and mathematics, can also be characterized by their very nature. For example, science and mathematics are dynamic disciplines that continue to produce new knowledge that either expands upon existing knowledge or, in some cases, negates prior understanding. Knowing the nature of the disciplines themselves can guide leaders' development of adult learning experiences that incorporate the essential characteristics of the content area.

One critical aspect of designing professional development with a clear understanding of knowledge and beliefs is the idea that it is not only the leaders' and professional developers' knowledge and beliefs, but also the knowledge and beliefs of those who are engaged in the learning. For example, if your science teachers do not believe that students learn through active exploration and engagement, then you have valuable information to guide where you might initiate adult learning, such as with an in-depth examination of research on student learning or of video images of classroom practice. Knowing the existing knowledge base and beliefs of the teachers and other adults in the program guides the design and sequence of the learning experiences.

◈ Reflection

As a leader, what do you currently know and believe about how people learn? About effective professional development? About the nature of the disciplines that teachers teach? About change and the change process? What more would you like to know and better understand?

What do you know about what other adults in your school know and believe? How do you know that? What data or other information do you use to understand what others know and believe?

In what ways do you use existing knowledge and beliefs to design adult learning experiences? How can you more effectively embed the knowledge base into your professional development designs?

◈ Notes

DAY 16

Professional Development in Context

We are learning that professional development that increases teacher knowledge is more likely to occur when such development . . . respects local knowledge (i.e., problems and practices that attend to the particulars of a context).

—Ann Lieberman and Lynne Miller

When it comes to professional development programs, "off the shelf" and "one size fits all" simply do not work for everyone. And there is a reason why these programs don't work. It is called *context*.

Skilled professional developers and leaders know they must take context into account if their professional development programs are to be successful. Here are the major factors that constitute context:

• *Students, standards, and learning results:* Who are our students? What are their cultural backgrounds? What standards are in place for student learning? How are students performing in relation to the standards? What achievement gaps exist?

• *Teachers and teachers' learning needs:* Who are our teachers? What are their cultural backgrounds? What are their prior learning experiences? How well prepared are they to teach challenging and rigorous content? What goals do they have for their own learning? What are their beliefs and perceptions of teaching and learning? How are new teachers inducted and supported?

• *Curriculum, instruction, assessment practices, and the learning environment:* To what extent are the written, taught, and assessed curricula aligned? How are content standards reflected in the curriculum? To what extent do teachers use multiple assessment strategies? To what extent do all students have equitable opportunities to learn? Are learning environments respectful of students and their diversity?

• *Organizational culture:* Do teachers meet and work together to solve problems? Are all school staff members focused on student learning? Do teachers collaborate and value each other as sources of expertise? Does the school embody and value the concept of a community of learners?

- *Organizational structures and leadership:* What are the decision-making structures and policies? Who makes decisions about professional development? What infrastructure is in place to support organizational changes that support learning? How are district administrators supportive of school-based professional development? Do teachers have opportunities to develop their leadership skills and abilities? To what extent do multiple school improvement efforts compete or support each other?

- *National, state, and local policies:* What policies impact professional development? What accountability systems are in place? How do policies impede or support collegial learning? What policies are in place to determine to whom and how professional development is provided?

- *Available resources:* What time do teachers have available for professional development and collegial work? Does professional development happen mostly during the school day? What is the allocation of school funding for professional development? What internal and external resources do teachers have access to? What community supports are available? What instructional materials, equipment, or supplies are available for professional development?

- *History of professional development:* What have teachers' experiences been with prior professional development? How have those experiences contributed to their current perceptions of professional development? What has been tried and abandoned at the school? To what extent have prior professional development efforts reflected what teachers and leaders know and believe?

- *Parents and the community:* What are parents' and the community's interests and concerns about teaching and learning? To what extent do they support the school's vision of teaching and learning and adult learning? How effective are the policies for involving them in the school's functioning, management, and professional learning? How well prepared are teachers and leaders to communicate with diverse populations? (Loucks-Horsley et al., 2003, pp. 53–78)

Context is obviously complex, with many interconnecting and overlapping aspects. Every context is unique. Professional development programs that are designed to match each specific and unique context are those that are most effective and successful in meeting their vision, goals, and outcomes.

◈ Reflection

Think of a professional development program in your school or district that worked well and one that didn't. What role did context play in the success or failure of the programs?

Think of a program that is in the planning stage. To what extent is context being taken into account? What can you as a leader do to ensure that contextual issues are being addressed?

❖ Notes

_____

_____

_____

_____

_____

_____

_____

_____

_____

_____

DAY 17

Critical Issues to Consider

Ignore the critical issues at your own peril.

—Susan Loucks-Horsley

The critical issues are the "tough nuts to crack" in designing professional development; they defy easy solutions. However, leaders and professional developers can be one step ahead simply by knowing to anticipate that these issues will at some point, in either the design or the implementation, play a role in determining the effectiveness of the overall program. An appropriate point to begin thinking about how to address these issues is during the goal-setting phase of the professional development design process.

The seven critical issues are presented here:

1. *Finding time for professional development:* How do you find ways to make more effective use of the time currently available for ongoing teacher learning? How can you work toward influencing state and local policies and public perceptions that more readily support time and resources for professional development?

2. *Ensuring equity:* Is access to the professional development experiences equitable? Does the design invite full engagement and learning by participants? Does the content of the professional development include the issues of equitable opportunity for all students to learn?

3. *Building professional culture:* Does the culture focus on effective learning environments (for example, learner centered, knowledge centered, assessment centered, community centered)? What do you actively do to build professional communities among teachers?

4. *Developing leadership:* Is leadership development a goal of the program? What do you mean by a "leader" and what roles do leaders play? What specific teacher leadership roles are important to develop? What other leadership roles are important for the success of your program?

5. *Building capacity for sustainability:* Do you develop people who can work with teachers to support their learning and teaching? Do you build support systems for professional development providers? Do you recognize, study, and apply the knowledge base of professional development theory and practice, and help others do so? Do you work to create and influence policies,

resources, and structures that make professional development a central rather than a marginal activity?

6. *Scaling up:* Is the program clearly defined and based on a sound foundation? Do you provide professional development opportunities to large numbers of people? Does each teacher have sufficient support to change his or her practice? What mechanisms are in place for quality control of the professional development for all teachers? Is there a plan at each level of the implementation for ongoing use, support, and institutionalization?

7. *Garnering public support:* How have you built public awareness of and support for the importance of teachers' professional learning? How have you engaged the public as participants or providers in the professional development? How have you engaged the public in understanding and contributing to your vision of teaching and learning? (Loucks-Horsley et al., 2003, pp. 79–110)

✦ Reflection

Think about a professional development program that you have been part of in the past. Did you ignore any of these critical issues? If so, what lessons did you personally learn about their role in the overall program? At what points in the implementation of the program did different issues arise? In what ways did you resolve the issues?

✦ Notes

_____

_____

_____

_____

_____

_____

DAY 18

Ensuring Equity

Students in low-income schools who need the best are getting the least qualified teachers. Closing the gap requires high-quality teaching and underscores the need for leaders to examine system policies, contracts, and practices that continue to perpetuate conditions of underachievement.

—Ruth Johnson

One of the most critical issues that professional developers must consider is ensuring equity. Given the growing diversity of the population in this country and the mobility of our society, understanding and appreciating diversity and being able to respond to it appropriately is an essential adult competency. Equity, in terms of access to professional development, is equally important.

There are normally three concerns related to equity that need to be addressed in any professional development effort. One relates to the staffing and curriculum of the professional development itself, another to the participants, and the third to the content of the professional development.

1. *Staffing and curriculum:* Is the professional development staff diverse in terms of race, ethnicity, gender, disability, and other factors that may be important to the professional development (for example, a mix of staff with experience at different grade levels)? Does the staff reflect the diversity within the participant group? Are the content, pedagogy, and materials employed in the professional development free of bias and stereotyping? Does the staff use inclusive language and promote the interaction of all participants?

2. *Participants:* What is the racial or ethnic composition of your participant group? Do both women and men participate? Are people with disabilities included? Are the populations that the participants work with represented?

3. *Content:* This aspect of equity is especially important when your program focuses on teaching content. For example, does the curriculum of your professional development address equity issues in either the content or pedagogy, or both? Here are some possible questions to explore:

- Which students enroll in the classes the teachers teach? Are they representative of the entire student body? If not, what limits access?

- How do teachers accommodate the diverse learning styles of students?

- Are there instances of bias or stereotyping in the texts or other instructional materials that teachers use? If so, how do teachers use these instances as teaching points? Are there bias-free materials available? If the materials are free of bias, to what extent do they reflect diversity? What types of diversity?

- How does the content affect diverse groups of students? Are there aspects of the content or the pedagogy that might be culturally inappropriate?

- What equity issues exist in assessment? Is one group likely to excel because of some factor or factors, such as bias in the test or testing procedure?

Those questions often provide an avenue into discussing the "undiscussables," such as, What do we believe about which students can or cannot learn? Do we discriminate against some students and not others? In what ways do our beliefs align with our practices? Engaging in dialogue about the beliefs, assumptions, and perceptions we hold about students, teachers, and learning is a critical element of ensuring equity within a professional development program.

In education, additional equity issues focus on when and where the professional development is held, whether teachers in schools in poorer neighborhoods have adequate access to professional development, which teachers get to go, and whether released time and/or compensation are provided.

◈ Reflection

What are the key diversity and equity concerns within your organization? How does your professional development address (or not address) these concerns? What do you think your professional development could do better in dealing with equity and diversity? How can you make that happen?

◈ Notes

Strategies for Professional Learning

New forms of professional development are needed for teachers at all stages of their careers—forms that can affect teachers' actions and interactions in the classroom and lead to improved learning outcomes for all students.

—Margaret Schwan Smith

Leaders need to have a diverse repertoire of adult learning strategies. Gone are the days when we automatically turn to the after-school workshop or hire an expert to come into the school and "train" our teachers. Currently, effective professional development is characterized by thoughtful and deliberate consideration of the existing needs, knowledge and beliefs, contexts, goals, and critical issues to inform the selection and combination of strategies.

Following are 18 different strategies (Loucks-Horsley et al., 2003) for professional development of teachers of science and mathematics, organized into six categories that offer a broad view of the strategies available for professional development:

Aligning and Implementing Curriculum

These three strategies emphasize using quality curriculum as the central focus for teachers' learning:

1. *Curriculum alignment and instructional materials selection* builds on established structures of adopting or aligning new curriculum and instructional materials to provide specific opportunities to develop teachers' understanding of effective curriculum, content standards, content, pedagogy, and assessment.

2. *Curriculum implementation* focuses teachers on learning the content necessary to teach the new curriculum, how to teach it, how to conduct the instructional activities, how to assess student learning, and how to incorporate the new curriculum into their overall instruction.

3. *Curriculum replacement units* serve as a stimulus for teachers to explore new ways of teaching and/or to implement several new instructional materials over time.

Collaborative Structures

These three strategies describe mechanisms for groups of teachers working together toward a common learning goal:

4. *Partnerships with scientists and mathematicians in business, industry, and universities* provide opportunities for teachers to work side by side with content experts to improve teaching and learning.

5. *Professional networks* are organized professional communities that have a common theme or purpose and emphasize sharing and learning from each other's knowledge and experiences.

6. *Study groups* are collegial, collaborative groups of teachers who convene to mutually examine issues of teaching and learning.

Examining Teaching and Learning

These four strategies emphasize teachers engaging in collaborative professional learning experiences to examine their teaching practices and their students' learning:

7. *Action research* provides a structured process for teachers to reflect on their practices and student learning by studying and researching their teaching and the resulting student learning.

8. *Case discussions* offer groups of teachers the opportunity to reflect on teaching and learning by examining narrative stories or videotapes that depict school, classroom, teaching, or learning situations.

9. *Examining student work and thinking and scoring assessments* engages teachers in shared, collaborative discussions based on student artifacts to reflect on and improve teaching practices.

10. *Lesson study* is a sequential and structured process for developing and refining lessons that are designed to address specific goals or standards.

Immersion Experiences

These two strategies reflect approaches to teacher learning that engage teachers in doing science and mathematics and immerse them in the content:

11. *Immersion in inquiry in science and problem solving in mathematics* is the structured opportunity to experience science or mathematics content and processes as a learner.

12. *Immersion in the world of scientists and mathematicians* engages teachers in scientists' and mathematicians' environments where teachers join in the work and fully participate in research activities.

Practicing Teaching

These three strategies provide opportunities for teachers to translate new learning and knowledge into practice:

13. *Coaching* offers teachers a one-on-one learning experience that focuses on improving teaching and learning through reflection, dialogue, and feedback.

14. *Demonstration lessons* are opportunities for teachers to engage in practice-based learning where the focus is on groups of teachers observing each other teaching lessons and engaging in pre- and post-discussions focused on a clear purpose.

15. *Mentoring* is a teacher-to-teacher strategy that entails sustained, long-term learning embedded within the school context.

Vehicles and Mechanisms

These three strategies are used as structures through which teacher learning is provided:

16. *Developing professional developers* focuses on developing the knowledge, skills, and understandings of those who conduct and facilitate adult learning.

17. *Technology for professional learning* refers to the use of electronic means of communication and delivery to support and expand on in-person professional development or providing distance learning opportunities.

18. *Workshops, institutes, courses, and seminars* are structured opportunities for teachers to learn from facilitators, leaders, or peers with specialized expertise. (Loucks-Horsley et al., 2003, pp. 111–251)

▧ Reflection

Consider the current professional development in your school or district. Does it implement any of the strategies listed? Which ones?

If your school or district has a more narrow definition of professional development, could any of the alternative strategies better help you achieve your goals? Which ones would work in your setting? What would you like to try and why? As a leader, what can you do to broaden the concept of what constitutes professional development?

Notes

> **DAY 20**
>
> # Purposes and Outcomes for Strategies

Educators diminish organizational creativity when they distort current reality through denial and minimizing and then they select strategies based on wishful thinking rather than a rigorous assessment of the strategies' ability to produce the desired results.

—Dennis Sparks

The professional development strategies are not selected or implemented in isolation or in a vacuum. The professional development design framework (see Figure 3.1) depicts the selection of strategies as the main influence at the "Plan" phase. However, all other inputs—knowledge and beliefs, context, critical issues—have continuous influence even at this stage of the design process. Additionally, what leaders and designers have learned about student learning, standards, and the vision and goals for the program also influence the selection of strategies. Every program or plan relies on a variety of strategies in combination. It's the only way to ensure that multiple needs, contexts, and outcomes are addressed.

How do professional development designers and leaders know which strategies to use? And in what combinations?

Often, four interconnected outcomes (Loucks-Horsley et al., 2003) drive the design of professional development programs:

1. Increasing teachers' content knowledge

2. Increasing teachers' pedagogical content knowledge

3. Building a professional learning community

4. Developing leadership (pp. 113–114)

Most professional development programs are, or should be, focused on reaching these outcomes. Obviously, no one strategy will accomplish all four outcomes, and programs will require a combination of several strategies. For example, a program that is designed to achieve these four outcomes might include some of the following strategies:

- *Content knowledge:* Immersion strategies, partnerships, workshops, courses, or institutes

- *Pedagogical content knowledge:* Examining student work, case discussions, curriculum strategies, or lesson study

- *Professional learning community:* Lesson study, demonstration lessons, or study groups

- *Leadership:* Developing professional developers, mentoring, or coaching

In addition to looking at the overall outcomes and goals of the program, leaders and designers can look at the specific purposes of individual strategies and the ways in which the strategies meet teachers' developing and emerging needs.

For example, some of the different purposes for the strategies (Loucks-Horsley et al., 2003) include:

- *Developing awareness:* Introducing learners to new approaches or content through strategies such as professional networks, demonstration lessons, or study groups

- *Building knowledge:* Developing content and pedagogical content knowledge through strategies such as case discussions, immersion experiences, workshops, technology for professional development, or partnerships

- *Translating new knowledge into practice:* Building on new knowledge and learning to plan instruction and improve teaching through strategies such as coaching, mentoring, curriculum implementation, or demonstration lessons

- *Reflecting on teaching and learning:* Examining teaching and assessment practices and student learning through strategies such as action research, study groups, lesson study, case discussions, or examining student work (pp. 113–114)

◈ Reflection

Think about a professional development program in your own school or district and ask yourself the following questions:

- To what extent was a variety of strategies included in the design?

- What outcomes or purposes were those strategies intended to meet?

- Were all teachers' needs and concerns addressed? For example, did the program include awareness-raising strategies for teachers new to the program? Opportunities to reflect on practice for teachers who may have been more experienced in the program?

- How would you now design that same program? What would you change?

▨ Notes

DAY 21

Practice-Based Professional Development

Learning about teaching in isolation from the contexts of practice is like trying to learn to swim on a sidewalk!

—Deborah Lowenberg Ball and David Cohen

Given the purposes and outcomes for professional development programs, how do designers and leaders identify strategies that will best meet their contexts, student and teacher learning needs, and result in schoolwide improvement and contribute to the overall learning community?

One approach to selecting strategies is to focus on those that embed teachers' learning in their practice, or are practice-based. *Practice-based* means that adult learning is "situated in practice" and engages teachers in "investigating tasks that are central to teaching" (Smith, 2001, p. 6). The content of the investigations is artifacts or samples of what teachers and students engage with on a daily basis, for example, teacher-developed probes and assessments with their accompanying student products. By examining student work and thinking, as well as the quality and intent of the probe itself, teachers have opportunities to embed their learning in their practice (Ball & Cohen, 1999; Hawley & Valli, 2000; Mumme & Seago, 2002).

In addition to artifacts of teaching and learning, teachers can benefit from reflection on and discussion of "episodes of teaching" (Smith, 2001, p. 11), which can include viewing videos of classrooms or reading and exploring cases of classroom situations and dilemmas. Episodes engage teachers in analysis and reflection on what matters most in teaching: What is effective teaching? What experiences best help students understand the concepts within the content? How do we know what students are learning and thinking?

There are several assumptions about teaching, learning, and professional development that underlie a practice-based approach to adult learning (Loucks-Horsley et al., 2003, pp. 160–161) and include:

- Teachers are intelligent, inquiring individuals with important expertise and experiences that are central to the improvement of education practice.

- The opportunity to carefully observe and analyze actual teaching and learning situations leads to changes in teachers' beliefs, attitudes, convictions, and, ultimately, practice.

- The learning of all students is a shared responsibility of all teachers.
- Improving teaching and learning is a long-term, gradual process.

❖ Reflection

As a leader, what would you need to consider in order for practice-based professional learning to work in your context? What type of culture and learning community would need to exist for this strategy to be effective? What structures or policies need to be in place in order to provide opportunities for teachers to have the time and support for this type of learning? What other strategies might be combined with practice-based approaches to extend teachers' learning and practice (such as coaching, networks, or study groups)?

❖ Notes

_____

_____

_____

_____

_____

_____

_____

DAY 22

Balancing Philosophy and Pragmatism

The professional development designer faces many dilemmas and decision points.

—Susan Mundry and Susan Loucks-Horsley

One of the basic dilemmas within professional development is whether to focus efforts on changing participants' philosophy about something or on pragmatic how-to issues (Mundry & Loucks-Horsley, 1999). As with most dilemmas, there is value in addressing both.

The *philosophical approach* focuses on learning theory and gathering evidence of learning. The *pragmatic approach* emphasizes new materials and practices, such as guides, methods, and curriculum, and other more practical matters.

If a program focuses exclusively on philosophical issues and research on learning, it is likely to ignore the day-to-day reality of making a new program work and may not be relevant enough for teachers who have immediate classroom management needs. If it emphasizes the daily how-to's, it shortchanges learners by focusing excessively on surface elements or the mechanics of doing something new without promoting real change in beliefs and behavior. Obviously, professional development needs both, especially as designers move toward sustaining the program and adapting it to the constantly emerging needs and changing beliefs of those involved.

How are professional development designers able to be sensitive to both needs?

First, there must be an infrastructure that supports a dual approach. Flexibility in scheduling is necessary so participants have time to reflect and interact with their colleagues. Sufficient resources are another requirement for sustaining in-depth learning over time.

Second, recognition of the need for integrating both the philosophical and pragmatic approaches is necessary. Many participants are more likely to embrace professional development that directly helps them do something specific. In our Leadership Academy we find it is most helpful to start with a specific example from practice such as engaging people in learning a particular lesson from the new curriculum, looking at real student work, or cases from the classroom. This focuses teachers on thinking about their practice and student learning from a very practical point of view. Then facilitators can help to guide the discussion to the philosophy or approach to learning that is embodied in the materials and the student work example. This raises the important discussion of philosophy of teaching but grounds it in the realities of practice and student learning.

In anticipation of sustaining a professional development program that incorporates both approaches, it is important to do the following:

• Maintain a balance between philosophical and programmatic approaches, and be responsive to changing needs in participants and the context. For example, combine time for teachers to work through specific materials they will later use in their classrooms, and then stop and reflect on what beliefs about teaching and learning are embedded in the materials.

• Gain agreement among participants about the focus for the professional development, and continuously determine whether the focus remains on track as the professional development initiative proceeds. For example, at the beginning of a teacher learning program, the teachers may want 70 percent of the time focused on the practical aspects of implementation and 30 percent focused on the philosophy and beliefs supporting the new approach. As time goes on, those percentages will flip, with teachers wanting more time to focus on why they are teaching a particular way.

• Build an infrastructure (funding, schedule, and varied approaches) to support both philosophically and programmatically focused professional development. For example, workshops and mini-courses can lead teachers to learn the materials they will use with their students; but they also need ongoing communication mechanisms, such as grade-level planning meetings and study groups, to have the conversations about how they are teaching and the philosophy behind it.

◈ Reflection

How do you design for and assess the balance between philosophical and pragmatic matters in the professional development for which you are responsible? Do you see substantially more of one approach than the other? If so, how can you create a better balance?

◈ Notes

DAY 23

Incorporating Reflexive Practice

How we learn is what we learn.
—Bonnie Friedman

One of the key characteristics of effective professional development is that it is *reflexive*. That means it is true to itself. It is internally consistent in its content and process. For example, lecturing about the qualities and characteristics of investigative mathematics teaching and learning does not stay true to the intent or nature of the content. Rather, participants should be immersed in learning mathematics by actively investigating the concepts as learners.

Professional development that is reflexive contributes to the overall adult learning experience and is characterized by the following:

- Participants who take the learning seriously

- An instructor or facilitator who is seen as credible

- Learners who regard the experience as practical and real-world oriented

- Teachers who have opportunities to apply their learning in their classrooms

- Participants who have the opportunity to practice new behaviors

Reflexive practice is sometimes confused with reflective practice, another important characteristic of effective professional development. In *reflective practice*, participants have specific times structured into the learning experience to think about what they are learning, its relevance to them, and what they may yet need to learn (just like the reflections in these contemplations). Reflections are important, too, but they shouldn't be confused with reflexive practice.

🖾 Reflection

Following are three professional development strategies. For each one, list what it requires to be reflexive. In other words, how would the learning experience be true to itself? (For example, professional development on outdoor education should involve some outdoor activity.)

1. Using various kinds of technology, such as computers, telecommunications, video, and CD-ROMs to learn content and pedagogy

2. Using structured opportunities outside the classroom (courses, seminars, institutes, or workshops) to focus on topics of interest

3. Working one on one with teachers in a coaching or mentoring role to improve teaching and learning through a variety of activities

◈ Notes

_____

_____

_____

_____

_____

_____

_____

_____

_____

DAY 24

Reaching Everyone or Scaling Up

Every child in America deserves a high-quality teacher. . . . Teacher excellence is vital to achieving improvement in student achievement.

—No Child Left Behind Act

As described in Day 17, one of the critical issues to consider and grapple with early in the design of a professional development program is scaling up or reaching everyone, and building a culture for learning.

Who participates in professional development activities? All teachers and staff? Those who volunteer? A smaller number who are hand selected? Who should come? These are not easy questions to answer.

In the past, one of the usual characteristics of change was that the staff generally had the option of adopting the change or not. Often, they could say, "No, thank you" to the new curriculum or new teaching approach. With current improvement efforts, there is a much greater focus on scaling up interventions to reach all teachers and their students.

The challenge of scaling up goes beyond providing the same experience to a greater number of participants. We know from the Concerns-Based Adoption Model (Hall & Hord, 2001) that people experience different needs surrounding the adoption of an innovation. (See Book Two, Days 4 and 5.) Providing for all these different needs in a single professional development event is very difficult. The "one size fits all" approach just doesn't work.

Mobility is also a problem. A core group of teachers can go through a professional development experience, and within a year or two, many of them may be working elsewhere. The result is very uneven implementation of the new program or practices.

What is needed to reach all teachers and their students is an organizational infrastructure and culture that supports a comprehensive and continual intervention. This includes a vision, mission, clear direction, flexibility in scheduling, and adequate resources. There also needs to be a human infrastructure built around a culture of learning, which encourages development of a community of practice. This is how a school culture both encourages and supports the entire staff to continue learning.

To have a professional development program that affects most people in an organization, planners need to do the following:

- Build an articulated culture that embraces change and ensures supportive policies and practices

- Hold high standards for learning and work to build a shared commitment to those standards

- Develop structures that assure new and newly reassigned grade-changing teachers the opportunity to engage in the professional development program (Mundry & Loucks-Horsley, 1999)

❧ Reflection

Is your professional development designed to involve all the teachers it needs to reach? What do you need to do to reach others? How can you begin to make changes in organizational infrastructure or human infrastructure to support a totally inclusive professional development program? What steps can you take to encourage the development of a professional learning community in your setting?

❧ Notes

_____

_____

_____

_____

_____

_____

_____

DAY 25

Team Learning

Team learning is not "team building" and shouldn't be taken on lightly.

—Peter Senge

Within a professional learning community that focuses on continuous adult learning, people often work and collaborate in teams. Whether these are teams of teachers engaged in practice-based professional development experiences, such as examining student work, or leadership teams facilitating dialogue about student learning data, there are specific skills and abilities that can enhance the teams' effectiveness. Leaders need to understand how to set up and support such learning environments.

Although *team building* is a common expression and is well understood, the concept of team learning is relatively new. Traditional team building focuses on improving individual team members' skills as a means for working with each other. It leads to improved communication, contributes to more efficient and effective task performance, and builds stronger relationships among the members.

Team learning is different. It refers to a team's ability to "think and act in new synergistic ways, with full coordination and a sense of unity" (Senge, Kleiner, Roberts, Ross, & Smith, 1994, p. 352). It is about getting a team to function as a whole rather than as a collection of individuals. Team learning begins with a high level of self-knowledge and progresses toward developing understanding of and aligning with other team members. It encompasses the traditional goals of team building but extends far beyond. It is one of the critical factors in building communities of learners.

The primary approach to team learning is improved conversation through dialogue and skillful discussion. These differ from normal conversation or group discussion in that they follow rules that allow team members to understand and appreciate the different forces at play. Because they don't necessarily come naturally, people need to learn these ways to communicate (Garmston & Wellman, 1999).

For team learning to occur, the following components need to be in place:

• *A task on which to focus and a reason for the group to work together:* This task becomes the practice field on which the team develops.

- *A facilitator to aid learning:* Team members become so engrossed in their own dynamics that there is no way for them to objectively analyze how they are functioning. A trained outside observer who can be impartial is often the best person to facilitate and give feedback.

- *A set of ground rules for their conversation:* For example, teams might develop ground rules that include telling the truth, sharing only pertinent information, limiting airtime, and avoiding blaming statements. There should also be ground rules for making decisions and for handling violations of the ground rules.

These are the prerequisites for teams to begin to develop the art of team learning.

▨ Reflection

Think about a team that you are part of. Write down several words that describe how your team currently functions.

- *Words that describe my team:* Does your team have a commitment to team learning? How do you know? What is the evidence? If it doesn't, how might you help influence such a choice on your team's part? What do you think your team could accomplish if it focused on team learning?

- *What my team could accomplish:* Does your current focus need to change to make the team learning more effective? How can you help your team move forward? Consider meaningful tasks for all members and processes to guide your work.

▨ Notes

DAY 26

Sharing Knowledge and Capturing Lessons Learned

A great cartoon in The New Yorker *some years back showed two venerable men, obviously scientists, sitting back to back at their respective desks. One says to the other, "It's just come to my attention that we've both been working on the same problem for the last twenty-five years."*

—Nancy M. Dixon

One of the ways to institutionalize communities of learning is for an organization to share knowledge and capture lessons learned. Lessons learned are key individual and organizational learnings—documentation of what works and does not work in a field—captured over the years. The lessons learned can come from research and evaluation efforts, action research, the work of experienced teachers, or the purposeful, collaborative work of a community of learners.

Often, neither the individual nor collective lessons learned in an organization are documented and shared. Education has been noted as the "closed door" profession, where teachers shut their doors and go about teaching and learning as each sees fit. Even when some sharing of knowledge does take place, reorganization and teacher reassignment or turnover can disperse those who possess institutional memory. Under time constraints, teachers may not seek out those with more experience. New teachers may not be sufficiently oriented toward the school's way of doing work. Michael Fullan (2001) points out that one of the key traits of today's professional is his or her willingness to share knowledge with others in the organization. The push for greater accountability has ended the era of the closed door.

Since capturing lessons learned can be difficult if a school is not oriented to the practice, here is an example that might help you get started:

Imagine that you are responsible for providing new staff orientation each fall. Over the years, you have kept a lessons-learned file that has several headings. One heading is "Scheduling and Logistics." Another is "Staff Benefits." Another is "Content," subdivided by subject (for example, District Disciplinary Policies and Procedures, Classroom Management, District Standards, Parent Involvement, Multicultural Issues, and so on).

A staff member who is responsible for setting up the orientation checks the "Scheduling and Logistics" file. There she finds some valuable information:

The facility you normally use is currently under renovation and is not available; in previous sessions, the staff preferred starting at 8:00 rather than 9:00 so they could get out early; and Chef du Jour has consistently provided the best food at the lowest price. Each file has similar information about what has and hasn't worked in the past—valuable information to those planning the orientation, especially those who are new to this function themselves. All files are electronic and are updated after each new orientation.

Another example of capturing lessons learned and sharing those lessons with others is when teachers engage in the analysis of data to guide instruction and student learning. Initial data analysis can help teachers identify students' learning needs and, after implementing interventions, data can inform the extent to which student learning increased. Documenting and sharing what was learned from the results of the intervention can be critical when other teachers encounter similar student learning needs and are looking for appropriate approaches to enhance students' understanding.

◈ Reflection

In your current role, are you sharing knowledge and capturing lessons learned. If so, how? Is this knowledge being used? How is it being documented? Are you sharing only logistical lessons learned or also instructional and school improvement lessons learned? How could you improve your efforts to share both categories of learning?

If you're not sharing knowledge and capturing lessons learned, how might you do so? What would your process look like? How would you be sure that your staff checks lessons learned before undertaking a task?

◈ Notes

_____

_____

_____

_____

_____

DAY 27
Using Program Logic Models

If you don't know where you're going, how are you gonna know when you get there?

—Yogi Berra

How do you know that the professional development you plan will bring about the results you desire?

One way to get the results you want is to develop a program logic model. A *logic model* is a picture of how your professional development program works—the theory and the assumptions underlying your program. "It is a conscious process that creates an explicit understanding of the challenges ahead, the resources available, and the timetable in which to hit the target" (W. K. Kellogg Foundation, 2001).

Although logic models vary somewhat in their conceptualization, here's an example of a classic model:

Figure 3.2   The Basic Logic Model

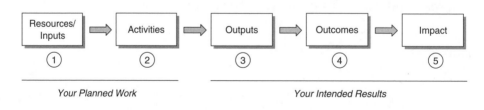

SOURCE: W. K. Kellogg Foundation, Copyright © 2001. *Logic Model Development Guide* (p. 1). Battle Creek, MI: W. K. Kellogg Foundation. Reprinted with permission.

Note that the logic model has two sections: your planned work and your intended results. Under planned work, resources (sometimes called *inputs*) are the human, fiscal, material, and other resources that are available for your use in designing and conducting your program. Program activities are what the program does with its resources—its tools, processes, actions events, and activities designed to bring about the intended outcomes.

Under intended results are the program's desired results: outputs, outcomes, and impact. *Outputs* are the direct products of program activities. For example, an output of a professional development activity is 50 people who have been instructed in using an inquiry approach to teaching science.

Outcomes are the specific changes in program participants' attitudes, knowledge, and behavior expected either short term (1–3 years) or long term (4–6 years). Following our example, an outcome might be that 45 out of the 50 teachers are using an inquiry approach to science instruction. *Impact* refers to the basic changes that occur from the program. No impact may be noticeable for 7–10 years, well after a program has ended. Using our example again, a reduction in teacher turnover might be a long-term outcome.

Embedded in a program logic model is a *theory of change*. It says, in brief, that if you have these resources that you use in this way, you will produce certain results that will benefit teachers and ultimately students in certain ways.

▧ Reflection

Although making you a skilled user of logic models is beyond the scope of this volume, here is a brief exercise.

Select a professional development event that has been scheduled, and develop a logic model for this event. Identify your resources or inputs and the major activities. Then list your outputs, outcomes, and impact. (You could ask a colleague to develop a logic model for the same event, but ask this person to list the outputs, outcomes, and impact before identifying the resources and major activities. Do you notice a difference in the resulting logic models? If so, what influenced the way in which the models were developed?)

What did you find? Are your resources sufficient to conduct the planned activity? Do you think the activities will produce the desired changes? Are they of sufficient quality, intensity, and duration to get you to where you want to be? Was it difficult to distinguish between, for example, outputs and outcomes? If so, don't worry; that will come with practice. What are the weak links in your logic model? What research supports it? What needs to be strengthened? What is the theory of change embedded in your model? How sound is it?

▧ Notes

DAY 28

Achieving Realistic Outcomes

I have become convinced that it makes a considerable difference if you do the outcomes before planning the activities. . . . I find that people come up with much more effective activities when they do. Use the motto, "plan backward, implement forward."

—Beverly Anderson Parsons

How do you know what reasonable outcomes to expect for any professional development program? Outcomes are synonymous with a program's results or effects. For individuals, outcomes may include changes in knowledge, attitudes, skills, and/or practice. For an organization, outcomes may be evident in changes in policy, goals, operations, or structures.

Sometimes, distinctions are made among short-term, intermediate, and long-term outcomes to designate when a particular outcome is expected to appear. Achieving intermediate and long-term outcomes is always more difficult because of the interaction between the program and its environment. There can be numerous intervening variables that can support, reduce, or nullify the anticipated outcomes.

One of the most common flaws of professional development planning is a mismatch between activities and desired outcomes. Usually the activity is not of sufficient quality, intensity, or duration to achieve the outcomes. Or to state it differently, planners overestimate the magnitude and number of outcomes that the activity will produce. You're more likely to be on target if you start with your desired outcomes and then work backward to design the activities that will produce the outcomes.

Keep in mind, however, that the process of identifying outcomes and strategies often becomes iterative. For example, once you clarify your intended outcomes and attendant strategies, you may find that additional outcomes may in fact be achieved through those strategies. Similarly, you may find several strategies could result in the same outcomes, leading you to condense or modify the strategies you offer in your overall program.

In most cases, acquiring new knowledge and skills and changing attitudes and behaviors require a sustained intervention. Having an impact on services or products requires even more time and effort. And regardless of how good a program is, the intervening environmental factors influence the outcomes, especially the intermediate and long-term outcomes (Kaser & Bourexis, 1999).

◈ Reflection

Think of a professional development program going on in your school or district. What is the specific activity or activities planned? What are the anticipated outcomes? For each anticipated outcome, ask yourself the following questions:

- Is the outcome best described as short term, intermediate, or long term?

- Is the activity likely to result in the desired outcome? How do you know?

- What is an estimated time frame for achieving the outcome?

- What intervening factors could influence whether or not the outcome is achieved?

◈ Notes

_____

_____

_____

_____

_____

_____

_____

_____

DAY 29

Gathering Evaluation Data

The potential of evaluation . . . is all about positive leadership, and it is only through that leadership, in its many forms that professional development will become all it must be.

—Hayes Mizell

Leaders are accountable for results. Leaders who promote learning in schools need to assess what the learning is and how relevant and transferable it is to the mission of the school or district.

There are seven levels of accountability that leaders may choose to examine when evaluating educational programs' effectiveness. They are as follows:

1. *Reach:* How many and what types of people were involved in the program?

2. *Quality:* Does the program's design and implementation reflect best practice in teaching and learning?

3. *Reaction and intended actions:* Were the participants satisfied with the program, and what actions do they intend to take as a result of their experiences?

4. *Learning:* What changes in participants' knowledge, skills, and attitudes took place as a result of the program?

5. *Application:* What changes have occurred in participants' practice and behavior after the experience?

6. *Impact:* What sustained actions have occurred over time that support changes in participants' behavior?

7. *Institutionalization:* What permanent changes in the learning conditions of the organization have occurred that support the continuation of the program? (Bourexis, Kaser, & Raizen, 2004)

Typical program evaluation usually focuses on reach (demographic data on participants) and reaction and intended actions (what the participants thought of the program and, maybe, what they intend to do as their next steps). Rarely has the quality of the program been examined nor the other levels of evaluation.

More recently, however, a shift has occurred. In addition to examining reach and reaction and intended actions, program evaluations have also added impact and institutionalization. This has been the result of a focus on accountability and a desire to improve student performance. The problem, of course, is that the program evaluators have skipped a few steps. These levels are sequential. One cannot expect changes in student performance until teachers' behaviors have changed. Program evaluations need to take all seven levels into account to ensure the quality of their program and its potential results.

◈ Reflection

Think about the typical evaluation of your professional development programs. Using the schema outlined, what levels are evaluated? Which are generally omitted? How would you redesign your program evaluation to document its quality and to gather the evidence you need to document your program's effectiveness?

◈ Notes

_____

_____

_____

_____

_____

_____

_____

DAY 30
Leading Learning by Example

Learning as a way of being is a whole mentality. It is a way of being in the world. . . . Learning as a way of being is a whole posture toward experience, a way of framing or interpreting all experience as a learning opportunity.

—Peter B. Vaill

An organization is committed to learning insofar as its leaders model continuous learning themselves, along with having organizational policies and procedures that support learning for all employees.

Such policies represent an organizational commitment to investing in human capital and being a learning organization in all aspects. This covers a range of topics, starting with a philosophical statement on individual, team, and organizational learning, to specifics such as employees taking reflection time for themselves; orientation for all new and newly promoted employees; and the sources and financial support for ongoing learning.

Regardless of what any written policy says, the behavior of the leader of an organization is the most important yardstick for determining what an organization truly values. If the policy says one thing and the leader does another, the stronger message comes from the leader's actions.

Here is what you as a leader can do to model your commitment to learning:

- Say you don't know when you don't know; don't pretend to have all the answers.

- Listen attentively and be open to what others have to say.

- Regularly seek out the opinions of others.

- When challenged, listen carefully and deal with the facts; try not to be defensive.

- Insist that all new and newly promoted employees go through orientation; do so yourself, if and when that is applicable. Know what the orientation of your staff entails and discuss that with them, as appropriate.

- Set aside reflection time for yourself and expect your staff to do the same. Also schedule reflection time for your group or team.

- Read and share what you read with others, as appropriate.

- Have learning goals for yourself and let others know what these are.

- Attend conferences in your field and encourage others to do the same.

- Support quality professional development for your staff and others in your organization.

- See mistakes and failures as opportunities to learn.

- Value staying on top of research in your field.

- Value expertise and use experts.

- Adopt a "problems are our friends" orientation.

- Subscribe to a philosophy of personal mastery.

Your adherence to these actions will convey your commitment to learning and to learning as a way of being.

Reflection

Reread the preceding list and check off those behaviors that currently describe you in relation to your commitment to learning.

How many and which ones did you check? How strong is your commitment to learning for yourself and for your organization? If you believe that it needs to be strengthened, what can you do? How can you help others demonstrate continuous learning behaviors?

Notes

_____

_____

_____

_____

_____

_____

DAY 31

Taking Responsibility for Learning

Words mean nothing. Action is the only thing. Doing. That's the only thing.

—Ernest J. Gaines

Modeling the way for others goes a long way toward contributing to a community of learners. Those who are leaders (and those who aspire to be leaders) are more likely to be successful if they take responsibility for their continuous learning.

Here is a 10-step plan (Reynolds, 2000) to guide you in taking responsibility for your own learning and, in the process, flatten your learning curve:

1. *Acknowledge what you want to learn and why you want to learn it.* Sometimes, you want to learn something because it is new, exciting, and offers certain benefits. Other times, you decide to learn something because you realize that you need to know it. To get to this place, you may need to work through some denial and acknowledge that you must obtain certain knowledge and skills that you don't currently have.

2. *Identify any negative feelings you have about learning something new.* Perhaps you are lucky to feel only excitement and anticipation about learning what you have chosen to learn. However, adults often enter a new learning experience with negative feelings. Are there any barriers that may keep you from acquiring the knowledge and skills you want? Are you afraid that you don't have the ability, the time, or the resources to learn what you have decided to learn? Do you worry about being perceived as incompetent or feeling uncomfortable as you learn something new? Simply voicing these feelings or talking them through with someone else can help to dispel them.

3. *Determine your motivation for learning something new.* Your motivation for learning influences your persistence and ultimately your success. Is there external pressure? Are you motivated by an internal desire? Perhaps both? Together, an internal desire and an external demand provide the strongest motivation.

4. *Make a conscious choice to learn what it is that you want.* You need to say to yourself or out loud, "Within the next six months, I choose to

learn. . . ." Making a conscious choice is much more powerful than simply saying, "Gee, I'd really like to learn _____ someday."

5. *To move forward, be prepared to give up your attachment to the old way of doing things.* We often are attached to the past. Giving up that attachment may be necessary before we can move on to learn something new. It may even be necessary to grieve the loss of the old before we can move on to the new.

6. *Back up your choice with a plan.* How do you learn best? How much time do you have to acquire new knowledge or skills? What resources do you need? Do you have them, or where can you get hold of them? Your answers to these questions are the core of an action plan to guide your learning.

7. *Establish some success criteria for yourself.* How will you know whether you are making progress or when you have reached your goal? Establishing one or two benchmarks can help you gauge your progress.

8. *Build in rewards for yourself.* Rewards are highly individualized, so pick your own. Maybe it is intrinsic—for example, simply completing your plan. Maybe it is extrinsic—for example, giving yourself a treat, such as a weekend away.

9. *Recognize that how you go about learning is an act of symbolic leadership that will not go unnoticed.* Others will observe how you approach learning and will learn from your behavior. You are a role model even though you may not be aware of it.

10. *Keep learning.* There is no end, and the pace is likely to quicken rather than slow down.

◈ Reflection

Book Three presents different aspects of learning and asks you to reflect on each. In addition, Day 30 lists a variety of actions that you, as a leader, can take to model learning within a community. Review all of the contemplations and select something that you need to understand or do better. Develop a plan for learning using the actions listed here in Day 31. To work on flattening your learning curve, consider a time frame that is shorter than what you would normally lay out for yourself.

◈ Notes

Bibliography

American Association for the Advancement of Science. (1993). *Benchmarks for science literacy.* New York: Oxford University Press.

Ball, D. L. (1996). Teacher learning and the mathematics reforms: What we think we know and what we need to learn. *Phi Delta Kappan, 77*(7), 500–508.

Ball, D. L., & Cohen, D. K. (1999). Developing practice, developing practitioners: Toward a practice-based theory of professional education. In L. Darling-Hammond & G. Sykes (Eds.), *Teaching as the learning profession: Handbook of policy and practice* (pp. 3–32). San Francisco: Jossey-Bass.

Bourexis, P., Kaser, J., & Raizen, S. (2004). *Evaluation framework for the center at IMSA.* Kill Devil Hills, NC: The Study Group.

Bransford, J. D., Brown, A. L., & Cocking, R. R. (Eds.). (1999). *How people learn: Brain, mind, experience, and school.* Washington, DC: National Academy Press.

Donovan, M. S., & Bransford, J. D. (Eds.). (2005). *How students learn.* Washington, DC: National Academy Press.

DuFour, R., DuFour, R., Eaker, R., & Karhanek, G. (2004). *Whatever it takes: How professional learning communities respond when kids don't learn.* Bloomington, IN: National Educational Service.

Fullan, M. (2001). *Leading in a culture of change.* San Francisco: Jossey-Bass.

Garmston, R. J., & Wellman, B. M. (1999). *The adaptive school: A sourcebook for developing collaborative groups.* Norwood, MA: Christopher-Gordon.

Hall, G., & Hord, S. (2001). *Implementing change: Patterns, principles, and potholes.* Needham Heights, MA: Allyn & Bacon.

Hawley, W. D., & Valli, L. (2000, August). Learner-centered professional development. *Research Bulletin, Phi Delta Kappan Center for Evaluation, Development, and Research, No. 27*, 1–7.

Kaser, J. S., & Bourexis, P. S. (with Loucks-Horsley, S., & Raizen, S. A.). (1999). *Enhancing program quality in science and mathematics.* Thousand Oaks, CA: Corwin.

Lindsey, R. B., Roberts, L. M., & CampbellJones, F. (2005). *The culturally proficient school: An implementation guide for school leaders.* Thousand Oaks, CA: Corwin.

Lindsey, R. B., Robins, K. N., & Terrell, R. D. (2003). *Cultural proficiency: A manual for school leaders, second edition.* Thousand Oaks, CA: Corwin.

Loucks-Horsley, S., Love, N., Stiles, K.E., Mundry, S., & Hewson, P. W. (2003). *Designing professional development for teachers of science and mathematics* (2nd ed.). Thousand Oaks, CA: Corwin.

Mumme, J., & Seago, N. (2002, April). *Issues and challenges in facilitating videocases for mathematics professional development.* Paper presented at the annual meeting of the American Education Research Association, New Orleans, LA.

Mundry, S., & Loucks-Horsley, S. (1999, April). Designing professional development for science and mathematics teachers: Decision points and dilemmas. *NISE Brief, 3.* Available at: http://wcer.wisc.edu/NISE/publications/briefs

National Council of Teachers of Mathematics. (1989). *Curriculum and evaluation standards for school mathematics.* Reston, VA: Author.

National Council of Teachers of Mathematics. (1991). *Professional standards for teaching mathematics.* Reston, VA: Author.

National Council of Teachers of Mathematics. (1995). *Assessment standards for school mathematics.* Reston, VA: Author.

National Council of Teachers of Mathematics. (2000). *Principles and standards for school mathematics.* Reston, VA: Author.

National Research Council. (1996). *National science education standards.* Washington, DC: National Academy Press.

National Staff Development Council. (2001). *Standards for staff development.* Oxford, OH: Author.

Owen, J. M., Cox, P. L., & Watkins, J. (1994). *Genuine reward: Community inquiry into connecting learning, teaching, and assessing.* Andover, MA: Regional Laboratory for Educational Improvement of the Northeast and Islands.

Reynolds, L. (2000, August 11). Continuous learning skills critical to career success in new economy. Available at: Kaplancollege.com

Senge, P. M., Kleiner, A., Roberts, C., Ross, R. B., & Smith, B. J. (1994). *The fifth discipline fieldbook: Strategies and tools for building a learning organization.* New York: Doubleday.

Smith, M. S. (2001). *Practice-based professional development for teachers of mathematics.* Reston, VA: National Council of Teachers of Mathematics.

Stiles, K. E., & Mundry, S. (2002). Professional development and how teachers learn: Developing expert science teachers. In R. W. Bybee (Ed.), *Learning science and the science of learning* (pp. 137–151). Arlington, VA: NSTA Press.

Thompson, C., & Zeuli, J. (1999). The frame and tapestry: Standards-based reform and professional development. In L. Darling-Hammond & G. Sykes (Eds.), *Heart of the matter: Teaching as the learning profession* (pp. 341–375). San Francisco: Jossey-Bass.

W. K. Kellogg Foundation. (2001). *Logic model development guide: Using logic models to bring together planning, evaluation, and action.* Battle Creek, MI: Author.

Book Four

▧ Leading Effective Groups

More and more leaders find themselves working with groups. The groups may be examining data and results, planning interventions, or learning about new standards. Whatever a group's purpose, the group is usually more effective when led by someone with facilitation skills. As organizations increasingly use teams to carry out work, leaders must apply the skill of facilitating effective team learning and performance.

In Book Four we provide strategies and suggestions for leaders who work with groups over time. Such groups have something to learn, issues to address, studies to conduct, tasks to complete, or problems to solve. Although much of what we say also applies to groups that meet just once or twice, our major focus is on leaders and their facilitation of ongoing groups.

A goal of all groups, if they are to carry out their work effectively and efficiently, is to develop community. One component of community flows from the way group members talk among themselves and to others outside their group. "Good talk" does not just happen. It is the result of individuals developing skills and agreeing that they want to interact with each other in very specific ways. The leader's role is to build an efficacious environment so that teams can do their work in a culture of respect and continuous improvement.

Material in this book was adapted from Garmston, R. J. & Wellman, B. M. (1999). *The Adaptive School: A Sourcebook for Developing Collaborative Groups.* Norwood, MA: Christopher-Gordon Publishers, Inc., with permission of the authors and Christopher-Gordon.

We raise important questions for a leader to consider: What does it mean to be a leader of a group? What are different roles for leaders in groups? How do leaders behave in these different roles? How do people in groups talk to one another to ensure effective outcomes? For example, what is the difference between dialogue and discussion, and when should each be used?

We ask leaders to consider even more questions: How does one plan and conduct successful meetings? What are the key components of successful meetings? How does a group handle decision making, when is consensus necessary, and when will a simple majority suffice? How does a group handle conflict effectively? Monitor participation? Give and receive negative feedback? And finally, how should a group evolve over time?

The questions in Book Four are grouped around four themes that are interwoven throughout the 31 contemplations:

1. What does it mean to be a leader of a group? What are different roles for leaders? How do leaders involve everyone and establish clear roles and functions for all group members?

2. How do people in groups talk with each other, engage in productive interactions, and build community? What are the "norms of collaboration" that contribute to groups' effectiveness?

3. How do groups make decisions? What are the different processes for decision making?

4. How do groups address conflict and problems? What is the leaders' role, and what roles and responsibilities do group members have for addressing conflict?

DAY 1

Leading Groups

When clear goals have been established and members of the team are committed to them, when roles have been assigned on the basis of strengths and everyone is clear about their responsibilities and the job they are to do, when surprising events are expected and responded to, when conflict is addressed, and when members work together, team formation and improved performance is underway.

—Roland Barth

What does it take to lead a group or team? Preparing an agenda? Facilitating a meeting? Creating environments conducive to sharing and learning? The answer, in each case, is a resounding, "Yes, and . . ."

Leading groups is not just about dissemination of information; it is also about creating "settings conducive to learning and sharing that learning" (Fullan, 2001, p. 79). Leaders have a responsibility to develop and practice skillful facilitation, arrange for the logistical needs of groups, and understand how to address and resolve conflict within a group.

Margaret Wheatley (2002) proposes six behaviors that characterize effective group conversations:

1. Acknowledging one another as equals

2. Staying curious about each other

3. Recognizing that we need each other's help to become better listeners

4. Slowing down so we have time to think and reflect

5. Remembering that conversation is the natural way humans think together

6. Expecting it to be messy at times (pp. 28–33)

A commitment to these behaviors can serve as the foundation upon which the skills and processes of effective facilitation of groups can be built.

◈ Reflection

Think back over your career and recall groups that you have worked with that were effective. What made those groups effective for you? What were the characteristics of the leaders and the members of the group that resulted in effectiveness? What did you do that contributed to the group's effectiveness? What did others do? What norms or ground rules guided the group's interactions? What can you do to ensure that these effective elements are built into groups you work with in the future?

◈ Notes

DAY 2

Four Roles of Group Leaders

Good leaders make people feel that they're at the very heart of things, not at the periphery. Everyone feels that he or she makes a difference to the success of the organization. When that happens, people feel centered and that gives their work meaning.

—Warren G. Bennis

What exactly is a group leader? Does this person actually direct the group's work? Help the group with its process? Intervene only when the group has problems?

The answer is, "That depends." Leaders have different roles in groups. Effective leaders know how to select and execute the right role for the right group and when and how to switch roles within a group.

The following are brief descriptions of each of the four most common roles for group leaders:

1. *Facilitator:* Being a facilitator is an appropriate role when the group's purpose is dialogue, shared decision making, solving a problem, or planning. The facilitator's role is to manage the process. He or she keeps the group on task, making sure that it does what it is supposed to do. This person is not the authority or expert and stays out of the content of the task, usually focusing only on the process.

2. *Presenter:* The role of presenters is to teach. A person in this role works with a group to broaden its knowledge, skills, or attitudes. A presenter can—and should—use a variety of instructional techniques and actively involve group members in their own learning.

3. *Coach:* Coaches help others achieve their own goals. At the same time, the coach helps colleagues strengthen their knowledge and skills in areas where they need guidance. Like the facilitator, the coach has a role that is nonjudgmental.

4. *Consultant:* The role of consultants is to provide their expertise to a group. Consultants target the content, process, or both, to help the group achieve its goals. To be effective in this role, the consultant must be trusted by the group and keep the desired outcomes foremost in mind. (Garmston & Wellman, 1999, pp. 27–28)

◈ Reflection

Think of the groups that you work with. For each group, what role do you play? Does your role match the needs and purposes of the group? Is this role the most appropriate one for you? Are group members clear about your role? How do you know?

Which of the four roles are you most comfortable with? Least comfortable with?

If you need to strengthen your skills in one of the roles, which one would that be? How can you increase your effectiveness?

◈ Notes

_____

_____

_____

_____

_____

_____

_____

_____

DAY 3
Group Norms of Collaboration

Most groups today aren't groups. In a true group all the members create the arrangements among themselves.

—Bobby Krieger

As the musician Bobby Krieger points out, it takes all members of a group to create harmonious collaboration. Effective groups establish and follow certain ways of functioning, which we call *norms*.

Different groups have different norms. Some may focus on how the group uses time, the roles members may play, or the conditions under which the group meets.

To have the kind of productive and collaborative groups we address in Book Four, group members must embrace certain norms. Garmston and Wellman (1999) have identified seven norms essential for collaborative work. They call them "norms" rather than "skills" because they see the actions as behaviors that *all* group members use. Thus, the behavior becomes normative, or basic, to group functioning. When these norms become second nature to groups, "cohesion, energy, and commitment to shared work and to the group increase dramatically" (Garmston & Wellman, 1999, p. 37), and a community exists.

The following norms address ways people talk to one another:

1. Pausing

2. Paraphrasing

3. Probing for specificity

4. Putting ideas on the table

5. Paying attention to self and others

6. Presuming positive intentions

7. Pursuing a balance between advocacy and inquiry (Garmston & Wellman, 1999)

Underlying these norms is an explicit intention to support the work that needs to be done and to develop the group and the communication skills of group members.

Garmston and Wellman (1999) suggest that regardless of the role a leader has in a group (facilitator, presenter, coach, or consultant), it is important that he or she model these seven norms of collaboration. If the leader is skillful in adhering to the norms, other group members are likely to do the same. And if current group members model the desired behavior, new group members will follow suit.

🔷 Reflection

Think about groups that you have been part of. Did any of these groups have a set of agreed-upon norms that supported their work? What were these norms? Were any of them similar to the ones listed ? What differences did you see between groups that had agreed on a common set of norms and those that didn't? How would you describe the differences?

Are there groups that you are part of now that could benefit from establishing shared norms? If so, how can you help this group? What norms would be most helpful to them in meeting their group goals?

🔷 Notes

_____

_____

_____

_____

_____

_____

_____

_____

DAY 4

Group Norm #1–Pausing

Listen or thy tongue will keep thee deaf.

—American Indian proverb

Group members, including leaders, are often so intent on what they are going to say next that they either aren't listening or fail to give themselves and others adequate processing time.

Garmston and Wellman (1999) point out that a speaker's pausing, or providing wait time, is essential so that others can process and respond to what has been said. It also gives you as the group leader the opportunity to reword in your own mind what others say to further understand their perspective.

People who are introverted normally require more processing time. They internally process what has been said. Those who are more extraverted tend to process externally. They are the people who say, "I really don't know what I think until the words start coming out of my mouth." The introvert is more inclined to comment, "I need some time to think about that." Keeping a balance, so that introverts have sufficient processing time and extraverts do not get impatient or bored, is a challenge for a group and its leader.

Key aspects of pausing include the following:

- Paying close attention to what others are saying

- Allowing processing time after a comment or question so that all group members have the opportunity to think through what has just been said

- Rewording in one's own mind what is being said

- Timing comments and questions so they are appropriately placed in the group interaction. (Garmston & Wellman, 1999)

◈ Reflection

Here is a brief segment of a group interaction. Read the exchanges and answer the questions at the end.

Group Leader: One of the criteria that we have to decide in setting up this scholarship program is, given our pool of money, how many scholarships do we want to award? Do we want to give several deserving students smaller amounts of money, or would we rather give larger amounts to just two or three students? In making this decision, we need to keep in mind other possible sources of scholarships, grants, or loans that our applicants may have available to them. Along with that, we need to consider our purpose—that is, to support students of color and diverse backgrounds who want to become mathematics or science teachers.

Group Member A: I think that we need to—

Group Leader: Excuse me, Group Member A, can we all take a few moments to jot down our thoughts about this before starting to interact? This is a very important decision we're about to make, and we want everyone's best thinking.

Group Leader (after a couple of minutes):   Okay, Group Member A, what are your thoughts?

Group Member A: I think that we need to give smaller amounts to up to 10 students. Investing all our money in just two or three students is too risky. We have no guarantees that they will actually continue with mathematics or science or go into teaching.

Group Member B: I think you're absolutely right. It's better to spread the money around.

Group Member C: I disagree. Our applicants deserve more support—

Group Member D: Yeah, you're absolutely right. The more support we give them, the more likely they'll stay the course and become mathematics or science teachers. Diluting our effort may deter them. There are no guarantees. Let's pick the best students and give them more support.

Group Member E: What kind of application do you think they should fill out?

Group Member A: I have a sample in my office. Would you like me to get it so we all can look at it?

Group Leader: Can we hold off on that topic for a bit and go back to our original topic of how many scholarships we want to give at what level? Group Members A and D seem to have captured the two perspectives. Can each of you be more specific by suggesting how many scholarships at what level you think would be appropriate?

Consider the following questions:

- Where do you see the group leader honoring the norm of pausing to facilitate group interaction?
- What are examples in which the group leader does not use the norm of pausing?
- If you were the leader of this group, what would you have done differently and why?

❖ Notes

_____

_____

_____

_____

_____

_____

_____

DAY 5

Group Norm #2–Paraphrasing

What we've got here is failure to communicate.

—Cool Hand Luke (screenplay)

Paraphrasing is a norm that Garmston and Wellman (1999) see as essential for group understanding. It is a restatement of something that has been said. The technique is important for the following reasons:

- It enables a speaker to know whether he or she was heard correctly.

- It honors the worth of group members by recognizing the content and emotion of their contributions.

- It moves the interaction forward through synthesizing or summarizing.

- It allows for correction of any vagueness, lack of clarity, or imprecision.

- It sets the stage for probing for details and elaboration.

Paraphrasing says to the speaker that you are listening, that you are attempting to understand, and that you care.

There is a logical flow to paraphrasing. First, signal your intent to paraphrase. Paraphrases should begin with "You" rather than "I" to keep the focus on the group member. For example: "You're suggesting that the group . . ." rather than "I hear you say that the group. . . ." Other possible stems include, "You're thinking . . . ," "You're wanting . . . ," or "Am I understanding you to . . . ?"

Next, choose a logical level with which to respond. There are three such levels (Garmston & Wellman, 1999):

1. Acknowledging and clarifying the speaker's content and emotion.

2. Summarizing by organizing and synthesizing discussion or by identifying themes.

3. Shifting focus to a higher or lower logical level. Going to a higher level happens when the listener connects what he or she has heard with conceptual ideas, such as goals, assumptions, or values. Going to a lower level happens when the listener anchors abstractions in the concrete by providing specific details he or she has heard. (p. 41)

Paraphrasing that summarizes or shifts the logical level of discourse can both support and challenge group members.

◈ Reflection

Here are five statements made by members in a group.. How would you paraphrase each one to honor the group member's content and emotion, summarize discussion or identify themes, or raise or lower the logical level of the discourse?

To help you get started, here is an example that paraphrases the speaker's content and emotion:

The comment: "I'm frustrated and angry. I spent two days preparing this report for our meeting, and no one has even read it. What kind of support is that? When last we met, you all were adamant about my having this report to you ASAP. What happened?"

The paraphrase: "You're obviously upset and rightly so. You've rearranged your schedule to get this report to us, as per our request, and none of us has read it. Your concerns are legitimate. Can we take a few minutes to figure out what happened?"

How would you paraphrase the following statements? Remember to start with *You* rather than *I:*

Statement 1: "I don't think this group is following its own norms."

Statement 2: "They won't like it if we decide to hold the professional development the third week of August."

Statement 3: "I think this curriculum is so much better than the one we're currently using."

Statement 4: "Implementing this new curriculum will be a breeze. Nobody will have any problems with it."

Statement 5: "I disagree."

▨ Notes

DAY 6
Group Norm #3–Probing

The power to question is the basis of all human progress.

—Indira Gandhi

As human beings, our utterances are not always complete and clear. In our interactions, we often need to probe, for a number of different reasons. We may seek data, information, or knowledge; or opinions, feelings, or commitments. We may also be looking for clarity, details, personal connections, past experiences, values, beliefs, or any number of other things.

The danger with probing is that it can often be seen as interrogation. Think back to when you were a child and a parent found evidence that you had done something wrong. Recall the string of questions hurled at you: "What time did you get home? Where were you? Who were you with? Why didn't you call?" Our probing of others can have a similar tone. At the same time, our questions are legitimate and move interaction forward.

One way of neutralizing the interrogation aspect of probing is by paraphrasing first (Garmston & Wellman, 1999). As you learned in Norm #2, start by using "You" instead of "I" so that you honor the person's content and emotion. This sets the stage for asking a probing question without being so threatening. Here is an example:

Without paraphrasing: "Why do you think that no new staff should serve on the districtwide committee? I think they bring a new perspective."

With paraphrasing: "So, you're thinking that we should remove all new staff from the group. Can you say more about how you came to that conclusion?"

What difference do you see between these two examples?

Another reason for probing is our human tendency to rely on generalizations, deletions, and distortions in our communication. These typical behaviors can lead to vagueness and lack of clarity. Comments such as the following are commonplace:

- "Do they have any there?"

- "I want to negotiate that with him."

- "That was the best meeting the committee has ever had."

- "Everyone knows that we tried that, and it didn't work."

So, what is the source of the vagueness? In the first example, the lack of clarity regarding *they, any,* and *there.* In the second example, just what does *negotiate* mean? What does *that* refer to, and who is the person? And what is "best" about the meeting in the third example? And finally, who is "everyone"?

@ Reflection

Here are the statements used for Norm #2. This time, take your paraphrase and add a question that seeks additional information that would move your group interaction forward. If you need help, here are some possible lead-in lines: "You're suggesting or recommending . . . ," "You seem to be thinking that . . . or wondering about . . . ,"or "From your perspective, it looks as if . . . ."

Statement 1: "I don't think this group is following its own norms."

Statement 2: "They won't like it if we decide to hold the professional development the third week of August."

Statement 3: "I think this curriculum is so much better than the one we're currently using."

Statement 4: "Implementing this new curriculum will be a breeze. Nobody will have any problems with it."

Statement 5: "I disagree."

Now, go back and review your responses. Are they more likely to be perceived as interrogation with or without the paraphrasing? How do you know?

Here are some examples of lack of clarity in language. Can you identify the vagueness? How would you restate the sentence for greater specificity?

- "What we need is more professional development."

- "We're working to improve our faculty/staff morale."

- "All children can learn."

◈ Notes

> ### DAY 7
> # Group Norm #4–Putting Ideas on the Table or Pulling Them Off

Good ideas come from everywhere. It's more important to recognize a good idea than to author it.

—Jeanne Gang

The ideas that we contribute to group interaction are what moves a group forward or backward (Garmston & Wellman, 1999).

Whenever we put out an idea, we want it considered because of its own merits, not because we ourselves are advocating the idea. (Advocacy comes later; see Day 11.) This is important because group members tend to react to ideas on the basis of their relationships with and opinion of the speaker, rather than on the merits of the idea itself. To separate ourselves from our ideas, we label them as *thoughts* and *suggestions*—for group consideration, not for personal advocacy.

Here is an example of how to introduce an idea. Declare your intention of presenting a suggestion to simply move the group thinking forward: "Here is one way that we might approach resolving the conflict we're facing." Another approach: "Here is a thought. How about postponing the conference until after the holiday so that . . . ?" Notice that this approach puts some distance between you and your suggestion so that it can be considered on its own value, independent of your status or position within the group.

Before putting an idea on the table, it is a good idea to ask yourself whether your contribution is relevant to the topic under discussion and if it will move your group forward.

The flip side of putting an idea on the table is taking it off. We do that when we have put forth a suggestion that no longer seems feasible or is blocking the group in some way. By removing your contribution, you take responsibility for your role in carrying out the group's work. And taking items off is easy—as long as you are not attached to your suggestion: "This clearly isn't a workable idea. Let's scrap it and move on to something else."

▨ Reflection

A Possible Scenario

The group you are leading is exploring ways to get 95 percent of the elementary teachers to participate in a series of professional development workshops on assessment. As the discussion moves along, you find you have the following to contribute:

- Prior experience in getting almost all teachers to participate in a professional development program

- An idea on how to motivate teachers to participate under this set of circumstances

Write down the way you might state your contributions so that the group is likely to consider them on their own merit rather than because you as the leader suggested them.

A Second Scenario

In this group interaction, one member contributes two or three ideas and starts advocating for one of them. However, the group is still generating ideas and has not yet begun to evaluate them or make decisions. What would you do to keep the group focused on brainstorming ideas before moving on to considering the ideas' pros and cons?

▨ Notes

_____

_____

_____

_____

_____

DAY 8

Group Norm #5–Paying Attention to Self and Others, Verbal Communication

Many attempts to communicate are nullified by saying too much.

—Robert Greenleaf

Being attentive to both verbal and nonverbal communication from oneself and other group members is another key to effective group interaction (Garmston & Wellman, 1999).

By paying attention to the physical and verbal cues in ourselves and others, we are able to do the following:

- Spot differences in people's beliefs, values, and communication styles

- See things from a variety of perspectives

- Use the nonverbal behavior of others to modify our own behavior

Attending to your own verbal and nonverbal behavior and that of others underlies all the norms. All seven are interactive and synergistic rather than existing in isolation. For example, when you paraphrase, you are paying attention to others and checking your own understanding. When you remove one of your ideas from the table, you are paying attention to others. When you recast something you have said to make it more precise, you are listening to yourself and making improvements in your communication with others.

In terms of verbal behavior, noticing others' words and matching your language to them is a way of responding to important data (Garmston & Wellman, 1999). If a group member uses a metaphor, picking up that metaphor in your own speech validates the other person and builds group rapport. Consider this example: A group member describes a project as a "wild roller-coaster ride." You continue this metaphor in the group discussion with references to "peaks and valleys," "breakneck speed," "gasping for breath," and other related references, as appropriate. (Exercise some restraint so that the metaphor doesn't lose its power.)

A more subtle approach is to match auditory words with other auditory words, visual with visual, and kinesthetic with kinesthetic. For example, a group member talks about hearing a number of "discordant" ideas being expressed. You respond by saying that you will try to "orchestrate" the discussion by identifying underlying themes you think you have heard. Your auditory word matches the other person's auditory word.

◈ Reflection

Here are some statements that contain metaphors. Read each one and decide how you might respond to the person making the statement by using or building on the metaphor used:

- "I feel that all we're doing is running around putting out fires."
- "That old building is sucking the life right out of us."
- "Managing information systems is like going over Niagara Falls in a barrel."

In this next set of examples, determine whether each statement has an auditory, visual, or kinesthetic image, and match your response to the same type of image.

- "How would you like to orchestrate our presentation?"
- "This project requires more assembly than I think we can handle."
- "Can you sketch out for me what the new plan will cover?"

◈ Notes

_____

_____

_____

_____

_____

_____

> ### DAY 9
> # Group Norm #5–Paying Attention to Self and Others, Nonverbal Communication

It's not differences that divide us. It's our judgements about each other that do.

—Margaret Wheatley

Because nonverbal communication—as exhibited in posture, gestures, voice tone and inflection, facial expression, proximity, and posture, for example—often carries more of the message than the words, being able to decode it is extremely important (Garmston & Wellman, 1999). That includes knowing what messages your own nonverbal behavior communicates and being able to read the nonverbal behavior of others. Remember that in instances of a mixed message—the words say one thing, but the nonverbal behavior says something else—the nonverbal is usually the stronger message and the one that is most clearly received by others.

So, how might you get more in touch with your own and others' nonverbal messages?

Let's say that you notice that when Group Member A introduced an idea, Group Member B stopped participating. She moved her chair back from the table, got her calendar out, flipped through pages, and made notes. She seemed to have disengaged from the discussion. You know her behavior changed, but you don't know why. Because total group involvement is central to your task, you want to find out what is happening and pull her back in if she has indeed left. That is an example of paying attention to nonverbal cues.

Note that in the situation described, you have not made any conclusions about Group Member B's behavior. You have just observed a change. You have avoided what Chris Argyris (1986) calls *the ladder of inference.* In the ladder of inference, a common human pathway, we select data, add meanings, make assumptions, and draw conclusions that often lead to incorrect beliefs and actions.

Assume that you had started up the ladder. Here is what might have happened. You thought you saw Group Member B look at Group Member A when he spoke. You thought the look was strange and concluded that there was something going on between them. Then, you speculated about what that could be. You ended up concluding that Group Member B had found

Group Member A's suggestion offensive and was upset with him. Note that you made all of this up. Your conclusion was not based on actual data that you had verified. All of this took place in your own head so quickly that you were probably not aware of the rapid ascension. And no one observed this mental manipulation except you.

Climbing the ladder of inference too quickly is a very common human activity and one to guard against in observing group behavior. Notice behavior, but don't draw conclusions before checking in with the person to see what he or she is thinking or feeling to confirm, or not confirm, your initial impression with verified information.

⬙ Reflection

Observe nonverbal behavior. In the next meeting you attend, pay close attention to your nonverbal behavior. Are you sitting or standing? Where have you positioned yourself within the group? What is your facial expression? What is your posture? Do you have any particular mannerisms (propping up your head with your hand, playing with your hair or a piece of jewelry, twirling a pencil or pen)? If someone were to walk by, what message would your nonverbal behavior convey? Is it the message you want to send?

If you are comfortable doing so, ask a trusted colleague who is also in the meeting to give you some feedback. See whether his or her perceptions are similar to yours or whether they are different. After comparing data, is there anything you would like to change about how you communicate nonverbally?

Avoid climbing the ladder of inference. Here are some instances that can easily trigger an ascent up the ladder of inference. What alternative explanations might account for the following behaviors? How could you find out what is really going on?

- A group member yawns a lot and occasionally closes his eyes.

- One group member rarely makes a contribution unless asked. Her ideas are usually excellent.

- One group member consistently arrives 10 minutes after you start the meeting.

❧ Notes

DAY 10

Group Norm #6–Presuming Positive Intentions

Change your thoughts and you change your world.

—Norman Vincent Peale

We serve ourselves and our group by assuming that others have the best of intentions and are speaking and acting out of positive motives (Garmston & Wellman, 1999). If that is the case, then framing paraphrases and probes with this assumption in mind is likely to keep the group on a positive note and move the interaction forward.

By assuming positive intentions, we reduce threats, challenges, and defensiveness. We also keep emotions on an even keel by not responding immediately when something bothers us. When we hear something that could be taken in a negative way, it is best to take a deep breath and pause, and then make an assumption of positive intentions. A deep breath and a pause can lead to reframing that is based on the assumption of positive intentions.

In presuming positive intentions, we ask questions in the spirit of inquiry rather than the spirit of interrogation. We also actively solicit different views and interpretations.

◈ Reflection

Activity 1

Here are the same situations given for Norm #5 in Day 9, with different instructions this time. Assume that each person is a professional who is committed to the welfare and success of your group. Using the alternative realities you generated for the reflection in Norm #5, pose a question to each person about his or her behavior that is not threatening, less likely to produce defensive behavior, and helps you clarify intentions. We use the first instance as an example:

• A group member yawns a lot and occasionally closes his eyes. A presuming-positive-intentions response is this: "You seem tired. Have you recovered from that hectic schedule we kept last week?" A presuming-negative-intentions response: "Is this too boring for you? Don't let us keep you up."

- One group member rarely makes a contribution unless asked. Her ideas are usually excellent.

- Another group member consistently arrives 10 minutes late.

Activity 2

Here are some statements that contain presuppositions. Identify each one:

- "If the other team had done what it was supposed to, they wouldn't be having this problem right now."

- "We're done with brainstorming. Now, let's go back and identify the good ideas."

- "Our previous leader should have cleared that for us before leaving."

- "If the agenda had been set up properly, we wouldn't be running over."

- "The books didn't arrive. Someone needs to call and let those people know what we think of them. They promised they would be here in 10 days."

▧ Notes

_____

_____

_____

_____

_____

_____

DAY 11

Group Norm #7–Pursuing a Balance Between Advocacy and Inquiry

When there is inquiry and advocacy, creative outcomes are much more likely.

—Peter M. Senge

Advocacy is attempting to influence others. *Inquiry* is gathering more information about options. Balancing the two involves spending as much time and effort on inquiry as is spent on advocacy. This balance is essential for individuals as well as for the group. This norm is the last because it requires the other six to achieve this balance (Garmston & Wellman, 1999; Senge, Kleiner, Roberts, Ross, & Smith, 1994).

Balancing advocacy and inquiry accomplishes the following:

- Respects the rights of an individual to join the dialogue or remain silent

- Keeps track of the relationship between advocacy and inquiry that is occurring within the group

- Surfaces the reasons and rationale for advocating for a particular idea or position (Garmston & Wellman, 1999, pp. 46–47)

One is just as necessary as the other. It is a question of balance and timing.

⬧ Reflection

Activity 1

Here are some pairs of partial statements of advocacy in which you are attempting to make your thinking and reasoning more apparent. In each pair, select the one that best communicates your thinking:

"These are the data that led me to believe . . ." *or*
　　"I believe very strongly that we should . . ."

"This is what is going on." *or*
   "From the perspective of an outsider, here is what I see."

"I've thought about this a long time before making up my mind." *or*
   "I've given this a lot of thought but only from my perspective. Do any of you see that I've missed something?"

"There is one part of this I don't feel I've thought through very well. Can one of you help me better define the problem?" *or*
   "If anything is true, it's that I do understand what is going on."

Activity 2

Here are some partial statements of inquiry in which you are asking others to make their thinking visible in a nonthreatening way. Again, choose the statement that is more likely to produce the best interaction:

"For the life of me, I can't understand why you think . . . " or
   "It would help me a great deal if you could explain your thinking about . . ."

"I think our underlying assumptions might be different. Would you be willing to tell us what you see as the 'givens' in this situation?" or
   "Our underlying assumptions must be different. I think the group agreed that these are the ones we're dealing with."

"You haven't said much, Harry. You're so good at reframing problems that I'd like to know how . . ." or
   "You haven't said a word, Harry. I don't have any idea what you're thinking or feeling at this point. Are you for or against us?"

"I think our proposed solution may go against the values and beliefs of some group members. I'd like for each of us to talk about how the solution does or doesn't support our values and beliefs." or
   "This proposed solution may go against some people's values and beliefs. If that's the case, so be it. They'll have to learn to adjust."

◈ Notes

DAY 12

Dialogue Versus Discussion

Communication leads to community, that is, to understanding, intimacy and mutual valuing.

—Rollo May

Not only are there more effective patterns of talk (as exemplified by the seven norms), there are also different types of talking, often with different purposes. These different ways are presented in Figure 4.1.

In this schema, conversation is informal talking in which group members simply exchange information, ideas, thoughts, or feelings with each other, often with no purpose other than to enjoy the experience. At some juncture, the nature of the conversation may begin to change. If it starts to take on a more conscious, deeper purpose, it has reached a choice point. Group members decide consciously or unconsciously whether the talk goes into either dialogue or discussion.

Figure 4.1   Ways of Talking

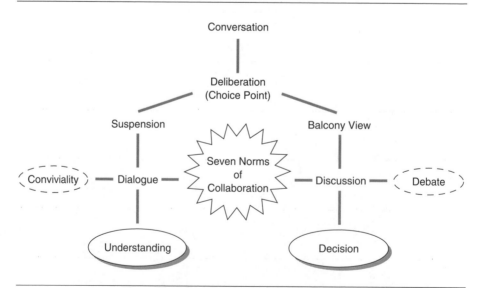

SOURCE: Garmston, R. J., & Wellman, B. M. Copyright © 1999. *The Adaptive School: A Sourcebook for Developing Collaborative Groups* (p. 52). Norwood, MA: Christopher-Gordon. Reprinted with permission.

Dialogue and discussion are two very different ways of talking, each with its own specific purpose and rules.

Dialogue is reflective learning in which group members seek to understand each others' viewpoints and assumptions by talking together to deepen their collective understanding. Dialogue often opens up the possibility of a better solution. The goal is finding common ground.

With dialogue, there is inquiry to learn and a desire to discover and unfold shared meaning, to integrate multiple perspectives, and to uncover and examine underlying assumptions. An appropriate discussion topic for dialogue might be the purpose and role of professional development in an organization.

The purpose of *discussion,* on the other hand, is to decide something. Discussion eliminates some suggestions from a wider field, with the stronger ideas taking precedence. In discussion, there is normally an action outcome. Most organizational meetings involve some form of structured discussion. There is a purpose and an anticipated outcome that moves the organization forward. In discussion, there is telling, selling, persuading, gaining agreement on one meaning or course of action, evaluating choices and selecting the best, and justifying and defending assumptions.

How one engages in dialogue and discussion has an effect on the group's productivity. In the schema presented, conviviality is dialogue that focuses on comfort rather than real learning. Debate is discussion that relies on intimidation and intonation more than logic and reason. Neither fosters group growth and development or productivity.

According to Garmston and Wellman (1999),

> At its most ineffective, discussion is a hurling of ideas at one another. Often it takes the form of serial sharing and serial advocacy. Participants attempt to reach decisions through a variety of voting or consensus techniques. When discussion is unskilled and dialogue is absent, decisions are often of poor quality, represent the opinions of the most vocal members or the leader, lack group commitment, and do not stay made. Skilled discussions take place when there is (a) clarity about decision-making processes and authority, (b) knowledge of the boundaries surrounding the topics open to the group's decision-making authority, and (c) standards for orderly decision-making meetings. (p. 57)

❧ Reflection

Think about meetings you've been involved in or led recently. Which type of talk happened? Was the talk largely structured discussions? Were the three elements of skilled discussion (clarity, boundaries, and order) in place? If not, how could you facilitate the development and use of them?

Did the meetings at any time degenerate into debate? Did they incorporate dialogue? Did dialogue ever slip into conviviality?

Was the type of talk appropriate for the purpose of each meeting? If not, why not? What could you have done to promote the type of interaction that best suited the purpose and desired outcome of the meetings?

◈ Notes

_____

_____

_____

_____

_____

_____

_____

_____

_____

DAY 13

Dialogue as Reflective Learning Process

He who differs from us, does not always contradict us; he has one view of an object, and we have another, each describes what he sees with equal fidelity, and each regulates his steps by his own eyes.

—Samuel Johnson

Dialogue—what makes it different?

Recall what dialogue is: a reflective learning process in which people seek to understand each other's viewpoints and deeply held assumptions by talking together to deepen their collective understanding. The goal is increased understanding—not a decision, not a next step, just greater understanding on every person's part.

The basic internal skill in dialogue is suspending judgment (see Figure 4.1). It means being open to what is happening in the moment and to what others are thinking and feeling. Suspending judgment also involves surfacing assumptions and beliefs, which influence our perceptions of reality.

According to Garmston and Wellman (1999),

> Dialogue creates an emotional and cognitive safety zone in which ideas flow for examination without judgment. Although many of the capabilities and tools of dialogue and skilled discussion are the same, their core intentions are quite different. Much of the work in dialogue is done internally by each participant as he or she reflects and suspends [judgment]. (p. 55)

The value of greater understanding is that it is the basis for conflict resolution, consensus, and community building. If certain group members feel they have not been heard, they can sabotage a decision. Dialogue ensures that every person is heard and, ideally, understood. "Working from a foundation of shared understanding, group members can more easily and rationally resolve differences, generate options, and make wise choices when they move to the discussion side of the journey" (Garmston & Wellman, 1999, p. 56). The seven group norms are extremely important for establishing effective dialogue.

⊚ Reflection

The reason this contemplation focuses on dialogue rather than structured discussion is that most of us are more experienced in the latter. It may be our primary style. We are skilled and comfortable. And that is important because effective discussion is a critical skill for group members. However, so is dialogue, but most of us are not as skilled and comfortable with this form of talking. Consider the following questions:

- How readily do members of your group engage in dialogue?

- How do you encourage people to share assumptions and their thinking on issues with the purpose of shared understanding?

Think of a problem or issue you are facing that you would like to ask your group to dialogue about.

- What opportunity do you see to use dialogue with your staff and colleagues?

- How will you teach them to dialogue?

- How will you structure the opportunities for people to practice dialoguing?

How can you establish a culture in which your colleagues are skilled and willing to use dialogue to develop more shared meaning?

⊚ Notes

_____

_____

_____

_____

_____

_____

DAY 14

Eliciting Participation From Everyone

An atmosphere of free exchange can be created only when participants see that a mutual sharing of opinions and ideas is welcome.

—Marion E. Haynes

In virtually every group, there are those who want to talk a great deal and those who say little. Ideally, you want to hear from everyone. As a leader, you may need to rein in those people who tend to talk too much and set up structures to encourage those more reticent to express themselves.

One of the basic tenets of communication is that silence doesn't mean agreement or consent. Unless people talk, it is hard for you to know what they are thinking and feeling. There are numerous ways to draw out people who say little in a group. Here are a few suggestions:

• Provide opportunities for group members to write their ideas and pair with another to share their responses, as well as speak in the large group. Some may be more willing to share a response after they have had the opportunity to write it down and say it aloud to one person.

• In brainstorming, have participants first write down one or more idea or suggestion. Go around the room, having each person contribute one item aloud. After all contributions have been written down, have another period of writing. Keep this up until you have a sufficient number of responses for your task.

• Set up smaller groups of two to four people, in which conversation may come easier for those who dislike speaking in a larger group.

• Extend your wait time so those who need time to think can do so before speaking.

You may also need to be proactive to make sure that some people do not dominate the conversation. For example:

• Establish a group norm about each member having his or her fair share of airtime. (This tends to keep the talkers under control more than it gets the reticent ones to speak up.)

- Say, "Let's hear from someone who hasn't had a chance to speak yet" before giving a frequent speaker the floor.

- If all else fails, take the person aside at a break and discuss the importance of hearing from each person and not having one or two dominate the discussion. In extreme cases, you may have to set a rule such as only one comment per 15-minute period.

Following these suggestions will earn you the respect of the group and, only occasionally, the hostility of one or two people who seem unable to control the urge to talk at every opportunity. It will contribute to group bonding—you with the group and group members with one another—and will help establish your group as a safe place to work. You will also be helping people monitor their own participation.

⊚ Reflection

Think about this scenario: By the end of the first session of your 6-week professional development series for elementary and middle school teachers, you see that you have a number of very extraverted people. Six people speak frequently, and about the same number haven't said a word beyond their introductions. Two of the outspoken teachers are from the same school, one whose test scores are the highest of any elementary school in the district.

One of your activities was a brainstorming session in which the teachers were asked to generate a list of all the algebraic concepts they thought were appropriate for students to learn at the primary, intermediate, and middle school levels. During this activity, you noticed that some teachers participated very little.

At the end, you asked for a voice vote on moving the time of the next session up half an hour. A majority said yes, so you adjusted the time.

In this scenario, what participation problems do you see? What steps could you take to balance participation? How could you make sure that you know what your more reticent members are thinking and feeling? How could you avoid making "majority rule" decisions that affect each member of the group?

◈ Notes

DAY 15

Cultural Inclusiveness

A culturally proficient leader influences others to make changes in their values, beliefs, and attitudes.

—Randall Lindsey, Laraine Roberts,
and Franklin CampbellJones

Any instances of bias and stereotyping in a group negatively affect group efficacy and can hinder the functioning of the group. Bias and stereotyping are violations of the norm of paying attention to self and others and can be communicated through the language we use. As a group leader, it is imperative for you to engage your group in recognizing, addressing, and "having the hard conversations" about any instances of bias or stereotyping.

There are six primary sources of bias and stereotyping in work groups. Each one and its impact are discussed briefly:

1. *Excluding people of color or members of one gender from group membership:* It is important to have your group membership reflect your stakeholders or constituency. A nonrepresentative group can raise questions among the larger community that can hinder the group's efficacy. For example, a question might be, "Why is that group making decisions about educational programs for *all* students when the group membership is not representative of *all* students?" Similar issues that surface within the group ("Why are there no women here?") can also negatively affect efficacy.

2. *Expecting an individual to speak for his or her race, ethnic or cultural group, or gender:* Often when individuals are a minority within a majority group, other group members will expect them to know and expound on, for example, the Native American point of view, the female perspective, or what Hispanics are likely to believe.

There are two fallacies here: one is that a racial, ethnic, or cultural group has a unified perspective, which is rarely the case. There will almost always be a diversity of opinion. Second, even if there were a unified perspective, it would be inappropriate to expect an individual to know and espouse that view. It is fine to ask, "What would our various stakeholders think of this idea?" It is not appropriate to ask an individual for the opinion of what the larger group may or may not believe, perceive, or expect.

3. *Expressing certain stereotypes or bias in assumptions made about group members:* Making any type of assumption about group members because of race, ethnicity, cultural background, or gender is another source of bias and stereotyping. Assumptions can be either positive or negative. For example, someone might say, "I bet you don't know the way to the Eastside recreation area. You live on the Westside, right?" Or "This is a good role for Jack. He can stack the chairs and move the tables before we leave. He's a big guy; he can handle it."

In such cases, you are, in essence, speaking for the person without the person validating what is correct and appropriate for himself or herself.

4. *Discounting another's contribution or attributing it to someone else:* A common occurrence in groups is discounting or ignoring someone's contribution only to affirm it when another person picks it up. Then, the idea is likely to be attributed to the second source rather than the first. There also is a good chance that the first contributor is perceived as a lower-status person and the second as a higher-status individual.

5. *Using jokes, puns, or other expressions of humor that reflect negatively on a particular group:* With the heightened awareness of diversity issues in recent years, this type of bias and stereotyping in groups appears to have lessened. However, it does still exist. Attempts to be funny using racial, ethnic, cultural, or sexual humor are more likely to be sources of embarrassment than sources of humor.

6. *Using derogatory language or offensive terms:* Referring to any group member using a derogatory or offensive term—publicly or privately—is simply crude and degrading. Moreover, it is likely to backfire. The news media have reported numerous stories about people who have lost their positions by making racial or sexual slurs.

The presence of any bias or stereotyping in a group usually indicates that the norm of paying attention to oneself and others is not being followed. Group members who don't realize the impact of their behavior on others can affect the group's efficacy and perhaps even the outcome of its work. It is the group leader's responsibility to challenge these instances of bias and engage the group in discussing the "undiscussables."

◈ Reflection

Here is an opportunity to practice. What follows are several statements reflecting bias and stereotyping made in a group. Imagine yourself leading the group: How would you handle the situation?

- "I'm sure that Leslie won't be able to meet on Saturday. I bet she has to take care of her kids."

- "I heard the best dumb blonde joke the other day. These two blondes were walking down the street. . . ."

- "Lester speaks Spanish, too. The two of you should talk."

- "What is the Puerto Rican take on this situation?"

How can you, as leader, heighten group members' awareness of the negative effects of bias and stereotyping?

◈ Notes

_____

_____

_____

_____

_____

_____

_____

_____

_____

DAY 16

Establishing Clear Roles and Functions

Nothing strengthens the judgment and quickens the conscience like individual responsibility.

—Elizabeth Cady Stanton

To operate effectively and efficiently, groups need to be clear about their roles and functions. It is the group leader's responsibility to make sure clarity exists about (1) how the group was formed, (2) which people participate and why, (3) the charge of the group, (4) how the charge relates to the organization's overall mission and vision, (5) what resources the group has at its disposal, (6) the time frame, (7) reporting responsibilities, and (8) how the group decides to go about its work.

Groups that are clear on all these factors are much more inclined to tap into one of their energy sources: efficacy. Members are more likely to believe that their group has the capacity to act and is willing and able to do so. The leader considers the parameters of the work, conveys them to the group, and answers any questions or resolves any issues that might be in the way (or works with group members to address unresolved issues).

One important step is for the leader and the group to set guidelines for how the group will go about its work. Here are some items on which the group should agree:

Logistics

- Meeting dates, times, and locations

- Structure of meetings (for example, agenda, time designations for items, distribution of written documents prior to the meeting, and so on)

- How to keep and disseminate records of the group's work

- Whether there will be refreshments and, if so, how they will be provided

How the Group Functions

- Determining roles for group members (for example, convener, recorder, facilitator, or reflector)

- Establishing processes for decision making

- Delineating guidelines for handling conflict

- Deciding how to handle issues of confidentiality and any conflict of interests

- Establishing limits of legal and/or fiduciary responsibility, if applicable

- Observing basic conversational courtesies: listening to each other, not interrupting, being respectful of each other, and carrying on one conversation at a time

- Specifying guidelines for giving and receiving feedback

- Honoring spontaneous humor and fun as the group works

- Determining how the guidelines will be adhered to or enforced

How Individuals Function

- Using "I" statements when speaking for oneself (except in paraphrasing)

- Notifying the convener (or other designated person) when unable to attend a meeting

- Being on time for meetings and staying for the entire meeting

- Responding to voice mail and e-mail messages within a reasonable length of time

- Agreeing to do what each member commits to doing or renegotiating the task with the group

- Agreeing to turn off cell phones during meetings

Although the group should decide most of these items itself, the leader sets a tone for how he or she wants the group to function by requesting that the group set ground rules and that members follow them. Again, this is an important step in building efficacy. Establishing these operational guidelines in a group is very common. What is rarely done, however, is to agree on how the norms will be enforced. All too often, established guidelines are ignored because there is no guideline set for enforcing the agreed-upon behavior. Members may feel uncomfortable pointing out inappropriate behavior, so that very quickly in the life of a group, the guidelines may be negated or followed only when members find it convenient or easy.

As a leader, you can make a valuable contribution to your group by establishing a process for ensuring that members follow the guidelines. This might entail giving each person explicit permission to alert his or her peers to infractions and clarifying the expectation that they do so—that is part of being an effective group member. In fact, in the early life of the group, you might want to practice intervening with members who violate the guidelines so your group will feel more comfortable enforcing the norms. Here is a place where the skills of giving and receiving feedback (see Days 22 and 23) become very important.

◈ Reflection

Think about a group that you currently work with and serve in a leadership role. In what ways have you provided guidelines for how the group manages logistics? How the group functions? Set norms for how individuals function within the group? What specific roles or functions need improvement? How can you facilitate and lead those improvements?

◈ Notes

_____

_____

_____

_____

_____

_____

_____

_____

_____

_____

_____

_____

DAY 17

Structuring an Effective Meeting

Ask any group of managers in any country in the world to list their three most time-consuming activities. Invariably, "meetings" will appear among the three. I have asked this question of more than 200 groups, and in every case but 3, more than three-quarters of each group indicated that half their time spent in meetings is wasted. The problem . . . is not being sure which half.

—Alec R. MacKenzie

Ask Alec MacKenzie's question, and you will get the same answer: unnecessary meetings, meetings that accomplish nothing, or meetings that go on and on. There is no inherent value in a meeting for the sake of a meeting. Every meeting needs to have a purpose, anticipated outcomes, and an effective process that involves all members.

Good group meetings just don't happen; they are the result of careful planning and leadership. One key is building a workable agenda and following it (Mundry, Britton, Raizen, & Loucks-Horsley, 2000; Scholtes, Joiner, & Streibel, 1999).

Here are some suggestions on structuring an effective meeting:

- Have a clear purpose for the meeting.

- Build an agenda around the purpose. Gather input from group members about the agenda. Others may want to add, delete, or reorder an item.

- Determine (1) which items are information items for which discussion is appropriate, (2) which are action items that should result in a clearly defined next step, and (3) label the items as appropriate.

- Decide how much time to allot to each item and indicate that on the agenda. You can negotiate more time if necessary, but at least you have a proposed plan for staying on schedule.

- Describe the process to be used for each item, including the domain of talk and the decision-making strategy (for example, majority preference) for the action items. Each topic on the agenda needs to have a process associated with it so members know how to approach the item.

• Place controversial topics at or near the beginning of the agenda. Placing such topics at the beginning of the meeting ensures that the group will have sufficient energy to address the topic.

• Distribute the agenda prior to the meeting. Group members need to have sufficient time to review an agenda and prepare for the meeting. They may want to gather data, read certain articles, or prepare a presentation.

• Before starting the meeting, review the agenda with group members to see whether there are any suggestions for changes. Incorporate changes as appropriate and then begin the meeting.

• Stick to your agenda unless the group decides to renegotiate items or time. Often, issues will emerge that a group had not predicted, and an agenda will need to be modified.

• Have someone take notes. Depending on the purpose of your meeting, you may need detailed minutes. In most instances, a page of action notes is sufficient—a listing of the next steps decided on and who is responsible for what. These serve as a record of the meeting and should be distributed to group members and others who need to know about your group's work.

• Conclude with a check to assess how effective your meeting was. Each group member could complete the following stems: "What I liked best about our meeting is . . . ," "What I wish we could have done differently is . . . ,"or "What I still feel unresolved about is . . ."

❖ Reflection

Sketch out a tentative agenda for an upcoming meeting. Distinguish between information items and action items. Assign times to each item as well as a process. Put any controversial items up front. Decide who will take notes and what type of notes you want. Send out the agenda beforehand.

At the end of your meeting, ask for feedback. What did people like and not like about the "new" agenda?

Notes

DAY 18

Providing Logistical Supports

Success is the sum of the details.

—Harvey S. Firestone

Good logistics won't save a poorly designed meeting, but a well-planned event or activity can be ruined by poor logistics.

Planning meeting logistics is beyond the scope of this volume. There are many excellent resources available that provide detailed guides to meeting planning. However, several aspects of logistics directly affect any group's ability to do its work and are important to review.

As a leader, you need to make sure that the following have been addressed to support your group:

- *Provide group members with complete premeeting information in a timely manner.* Your event can get off to a shaky start if members have not been informed about time, place, parking, agenda, and other logistical aspects of the meeting. Informing your members enables them to come prepared to do the group's work.

- *Select a room that is appropriate for the group's work.* Not any vacant room will do. The room needs to accommodate the work the group is doing. That includes the configuration of space, access to natural light, the positioning of the table and chairs, and the acoustics.

- *Provide appropriate materials for the group's work.* These may include audiovisual aids; computers; charting materials; and prepared reference materials, handouts, or worksheets. Print materials need to be error free and look professional. There must be adequate space on the walls for putting up posters or flip chart sheets to help the group track its work.

- *Arrange for refreshments.* Groups can work more effectively if they have ready access to food and drink for the duration of their event. Unless you start a meeting right after a meal, it is a good idea to have food and drink available at the beginning of a meeting rather than halfway through or at the end.

- *Plan the agenda so that members can make a transition into the meeting.* People often come into a meeting with the day's events—rather than the meeting—primary in their minds. They may be thinking about a conflict they are having, the report they are working on, or getting to a meeting after this one. If you structure a transition activity at the beginning, you will help members focus on the immediate situation. One way of doing that is to pose the question, "What is foremost in your mind right now that you want to put on hold for the next two hours, and what are your expectations for this meeting?" Having each person respond can make the transition, and you can then proceed with your agenda.

◈ Reflection

Think about your next meeting coming up. Have all these logistical supports been provided for? If not, what do you need to attend to? What moves can you make as the facilitator to better ensure that group members participate fully?

◈ Notes

_____

_____

_____

_____

_____

_____

_____

DAY 19

Setting Up the Meeting Room

When facilities are proper, they go unnoticed.

—Marion E. Haynes

What do you do when company comes to visit? Clean the house? Make sure the guest room is ready? Make a trip to the grocery? Ask the kids to put their toys away?

These are typical ways in which we prepare to welcome our guests and make them comfortable. But how many of us do this for our meetings? It is what David Perkins (1992) calls defining the *surround.* The surround is comprised of the features that influence thought and action in a group. These may be psychological, emotional, cognitive, or physical in nature. As a group leader, you have some influence on all of these, but you have the most control over the physical features of the meeting room.

What is important to know about the physical features? Here are some points to remember (Garmston & Wellman, 1999):

• *Everyone should be able to see and hear each other.* There are many different seating arrangements for groups of all sizes: semicircle, horseshoe shape, and so on. Depending on the acoustics, a group of 40 or more may require amplification.

• *Every participant should be able to see the group leader and the flip chart, screen, or other visual aids.* Seeing visual aids and the facilitator is essential for the group to proceed with the work. Participants should face away from the door or entryways.

• *The chairs and tables (if used) should be appropriate for the size of the group.* Extra tables and chairs that are not used disturb the energy balance in the room and should be removed. Taking out empty chairs allows for a more direct group connection.

• *The arrangement of the room should allow for individual movement and for subgroupings; participants need to see the whole room as their space rather than restrict themselves to a particular chair.* People have a tendency to select the same seats in meetings. Changing seats produces more energy in the room and gives participants a different perspective.

• *Tools for helping the group with its work (for example, flip charts, white boards, or other recording devices) should document the group's work.* Certain tasks such as planning, problem solving, and decision making require access to data as well as charting materials. Being able to post written materials on the wall and write on flip charts is critical to a group's work.

• *In setting up the room, provide different areas where the facilitator can be strategically positioned to lead the group.* For example, one of the facilitator's jobs is to give instructions, and that can best be done by communicating in three different mediums: space, voice, and language. In giving directions, the facilitator selects a key spot, uses a credible voice that elicits support, and gives the directions. Then, he or she moves to a different place and checks for understanding, using a softer, more approachable voice. The facilitator has now established a physical space in which he or she can change roles, from checking in with group members to correcting and clarifying behaviors. (Garmston & Wellman, 1999)

☒ Reflection

Activity 1

Think of a recent meeting that you attended. Recall the room arrangement. Did it satisfy the following criteria? Did it:

• Allow participants to see each other?

• Enable participants to see the facilitator and any visual aids?

• Seat nonparticipants separately from participants?

• Match the chairs to the number of participants?

• Have sufficient room for people to move around?

• Have adequate tools to support the meeting?

If there was something amiss, what could you do to correct it for the next meeting?

Activity 2

Recall the last time you gave directions to a group. How did you do so? Did you use your physical space effectively to reinforce communication as described above? What would you do differently in the future?

◈ Notes

DAY 20

Group Decision Making

The word decide *means to kill choice: Out of many options, the group selects some ideas to survive and others to be set aside.*

—Robert Garmston and Bruce Wellman

Many groups get stuck because they are not sure how to make a decision.

There are many ways a group can go about its decision making. Actually, the way a group makes a decision may depend on the nature of the decision to be made. Not all decisions require the same amount or base of support. Some need a lot; others need much less.

Here are five major ways that a group may make a decision:

1. By full consensus

2. By "sufficient consensus" (see Day 21)

3. By a majority vote

4. By delegating the decision to a subgroup

5. By delegating the decision to an individual group member

For any of these decision-making options, the full decision may lie with the group or some part of the group, or the group may solicit input from nongroup members, such as other staff members, administrators, or stakeholders.

Generally, the more a decision requires commitment to any kind of collective action, the more broadly based the decision needs to be.

◈ Reflection

Here are some decisions that a group might be making. Using the approaches listed, how should each be made? Recognize that the approach you use may well depend on the context, and that may generate alternative approaches:

• Set a date for the next group meeting.

• Select a new group leader.

- Determine the focus of the next professional development program.

- Recommend a new curriculum.

- Decide what color and type of folders to use in the next professional development activity.

Think about the groups you are currently leading. Are the members in each of them clear about how they make decisions? Do they make decisions in different ways depending on the level of commitment needed? If your answer to either question is "No," what can you do to strengthen their abilities to use appropriate decision-making processes?

◈ Notes

_____

_____

_____

_____

_____

_____

_____

_____

_____

DAY 21

Reaching Consensus

A genuine leader is not a searcher for consensus but a molder of consensus.
— Martin Luther King, Jr.

Groups often talk about wanting consensus, but consensus is very hard to achieve, and in many instances, it is simply not necessary. Some decisions don't require that broad a base of support. Some groups are not constituted in a way that makes consensus possible. In other instances, they may not have the time or resources to push for a full consensus.

For most groups, what Garmston and Wellman (1999) call *sufficient consensus* is enough. Sufficient consensus means that at least 80 percent of the group agrees and are prepared to act. The remaining 20 percent may not concur, but they have agreed not to sabotage the action. They are not in agreement, but they can live with the decision—whatever it may be.

However, if full consensus is required of a group, Garmston and Wellman (1999) provide a list of conditions that need to be present before a full consensus is possible:

• There should be clarity about the group's purpose and how it operates.

• Power in the group needs to be distributed equally. Consensus doesn't work in hierarchical groups.

• The group needs to have the autonomy to choose consensus. A group may find it difficult to reach full consensus if it is getting pressured to make a decision and move on.

• Consensus requires a great deal of time and patience, which a group may not have.

• Group members must be willing to spend time examining their own functioning.

• Individual group members must be willing to reflect on their own thinking and be open to change.

• Group members and the group as a whole must continually sharpen communication, participation, and facilitation skills. (pp. 58–59)

◈ Reflection

With this list of the requirements for effective consensus building and the caveat of sufficient consensus in mind, think of the groups you lead.

Are any structured for consensus building? If so, which ones? How do you know? What types of decisions might they be making in which a full consensus is necessary? For what types of decisions would a sufficient consensus be more appropriate? As a group leader, how do you establish the structures and conditions within a group for consensus building?

Here is a reminder: Effective groups don't always use consensus; their decisions depend on the situation. More consensus building is not always necessary or even desirable.

◈ Notes

_____

_____

_____

_____

_____

_____

_____

_____

DAY 22

Giving Negative Feedback

The two words "information" and "communication" are often used interchangeably, but they signify quite different things. Information is "giving out"; communication is "getting through."

—Sydney J. Harris

Effective groups are skilled at giving and receiving feedback. This is one way in which groups learn and are able to make course corrections. Feedback is absolutely essential if individuals and their groups and organization are to grow and develop. In fact, exchanging feedback should become part of an organization's culture. Giving and receiving feedback should be as common as getting a new assignment. It is simply part of how a group or an organization functions.

What follows are some ground rules for giving and receiving negative feedback. Why only negative? Because giving positive feedback is easy. Most people welcome positive feedback. The negative is trickier.

Giving Feedback

The context: Negative feedback should be accompanied by feedback on what is going well. There is a tendency to provide feedback only when there is a problem, thus making the feedback largely negative. Knowing what they are doing well is as important for people as knowing what they need to improve on.

The timing of feedback is critical, as well as the circumstances under which it is delivered. It is normally not a good idea to give negative feedback by e-mail or voice mail. The nonverbal communication channel is largely absent, and your message can easily be misconstrued. Also, the person may receive the message at an inappropriate time.

Also, avoid giving negative feedback when you or the other person is feeling strong emotions or when either of you is experiencing low self-esteem. Don't give feedback when the other person is leaving, can't do anything to correct the problem, or when the physical setting is inappropriate. Avoid "gotchas" that focus on all the things the person has done wrong. Make sure your feedback is on target and is useful to the other person.

The delivery: Always speak first for yourself—not for other people—even if you know others feel the same way. Describe the behavior as objectively as possible, without using labels. Don't exaggerate or be judgmental. Keep your feedback to the facts you know firsthand. Help people hear and accept your compliments. In the midst of your negative feedback, they may not focus on the positives you convey.

The sequence: Here are six key stems for you to complete in delivering constructive feedback:

1. "When you _____"
2. "I feel _____"
3. "Because I _____."

Provide a time out for the other person to respond to what you have said. Then continue with:

4. "I would like _____"
5. "Because _____."
6. "What do you think?"

Provide another opportunity for the person to react. Here is an example: "When you come to group meetings without your assignments completed, I feel let down and angry. It keeps us from getting our work done in a timely fashion. You are pulling us off our time schedule. [Pause for discussion.] I would like you to have your work done at the beginning of each meeting. That way, we're much more likely to adhere to our time frame. What do you think?"

◈ Reflection

Think of a team member to whom you would like to give some negative feedback about his or her behavior. Write that feedback down on a sheet of paper.

Now, go back and review it against the criteria listed. To what degree does your feedback follow the guidelines? What changes will you make?

▨ Notes

_____

_____

_____

_____

_____

_____

_____

_____

_____

_____

_____

_____

DAY 23

Receiving Negative Feedback

Evaluation and especially self-evaluation are highly and positively related to learning. Evaluation is no less important than encouragement. Feedback, including negative feedback, is essential for human growth.

—Roland Barth

The other side of giving negative feedback is receiving negative feedback.

Receiving Feedback

The context: You are likely to find yourself receiving negative feedback from someone who may not be skilled in following the guidelines suggested in Day 22. If that is the case, you may be able to help the deliverer recast the feedback so it corresponds more closely to those guidelines. If that doesn't work, you may simply have to listen to what the person has to say and work your way through.

Here are some suggestions to help you receive negative feedback:

First and foremost, breathe. When you are hearing things you may not want to hear, it is normal to tense and tighten your muscles and start breathing shallowly. Try to take deep breaths so your brain gets sufficient oxygen. Listen carefully, without interrupting, to what the person has to say. Ask for clarity or for specific examples. (Scholtes et al., 1999)

After the other person has made his or her major point, paraphrase the message to acknowledge the speaker and to make sure you have heard correctly. At this point, you are just checking for understanding. Next, agree with whatever the person has said that is true. This may require suppressing your ego and its normal defensive reaction. For example, agree to the fact that you failed to notify three important people about a meeting, if that is what you did.

If you didn't do what your colleague says you did, speak up—again, in a nondefensive manner. Say something such as, "I understand that you think

I failed to notify those three people about the meeting. I see it differently. Here is my understanding of what happened. . . ." This is also a good point in the conversation to put any documentation you have concerning the issue between you and your colleague; this creates the "third point" (see Day 24).

Don't rush into resolution unless the desired solution is readily apparent. Perhaps an apology is in order. If so, you can apologize, identify what you are apologizing for, and state what you will or won't do as resolution. Or perhaps you need time to think something over. If so, tell your colleague that you need some time and let her know when you will get back to her; and then keep your commitment.

◈ Reflection

Think back to a recent time someone gave you negative feedback. How did you respond? Were you able to listen? Were you able to admit that you acted inappropriately, if that was the case? Did you feel yourself getting defensive? If so, how did you know? What were the clues? Was the situation resolved? If so, how? What could you have done differently?

As a leader, how can you help your group members understand and follow the guidelines for giving and receiving negative feedback?

◈ Notes

_____

_____

_____

_____

_____

_____

DAY 24

Sharing Unpleasant
or Negative Information

*People love to talk but hate to listen. Listening is not merely not talking.
. . . It means taking a vigorous, human interest in what is being told to
us. You can listen like a blank wall or like a splendid auditorium where
every sound comes back fuller and richer.*

—Alice Duer Miller

How do you go about sharing unpleasant or negative information in a positive and constructive way? How do you engage the recipient in focusing on
the topic and not on you as the "messenger" of the news?

Sharing negative information is not the same as giving negative feedback
(see Day 22). Negative feedback should always be given in a private, one on
one context. Sharing negative information, on the other hand, can happen
in a more public and larger group context.

A series of specific steps called "How Not to Get Shot" (HNTGS) is
Michael Grinder's (1998) strategy for allowing your audience to disassociate
you from the negative news that you deliver. The purpose of HNTGS is to
create a space and time for a group to grapple with difficult issues and still
preserve professional relationships. It's a strategy that enables both the messenger and the recipient to focus on the issue in front of them and not on
interpersonal issues. In her book, *Leadership and the New Science* (1992),
Margaret Wheatley stresses the association between energy and relationships and how solutions emerge from the relationships among people.
HNTGS is one way to maintain the energy of relationships and not let the
negative topic interfere with the solutions. It is also a strategy that relies on
both verbal and nonverbal communication.

Here is a description of each of the HNTGS steps:

• *Go visual.* Information delivered orally makes the group dependent on
the person delivering the information. If someone does not hear it, the information will need to be repeated. Information displayed visually on a flip
chart allows group members to look at it as they choose and process it in
their own time frame. In other words, having a visual display makes the
participants less dependent on the messenger.

- *Get it off to the side.* The messenger can facilitate communication by separating issues from solutions and creating situations in which group members can grapple with difficult issues and still maintain relationships. Once the information is displayed visually, "get it off to the side" to create a "third point." The messenger and group can then focus on this additional point in examining the issues rather than having "two-point" communication, directly between the leader and the group members.

- *Redirect the group's attention.* Because group members follow the messenger's eyes, use this to redirect their attention to the visual message. For example, make a "frozen hand" gesture toward the group and then move the hand toward the visual message. At the same time, the messenger should turn his or her head and eyes in coordination with the hand gesture. When the group looks at the visual message, the messenger can then look at the group to read people's nonverbal reactions. This sets the stage for the messenger to be proactive in facilitating a group toward its desired outcomes.

- *In speaking, avoid possessive modifiers.* Instead of saying "my report" or "my schedule," talk about "the report" or "the schedule." Neutral modifiers decrease defensiveness and the attribution of blame. This helps to maintain relationships.

- *Separate the location of the problem from the location of the solution.* This suggestion is predicated on the idea that locations have memory—whether positive or negative. For example, do you remember where you were when President Kennedy was assassinated or when the terrorist attacks on September 11, 2001, occurred? Using separate locations allows the messenger to preserve relationships by creating one physical location for problems or issues and a separate location for the solutions. For example, if you are delivering "bad news, do so from one spot in the room, and then move to another spot in the room to engage the group in problem solving or brainstorming for solutions.

- *Use an approachable voice.* The messenger chooses voice tone very carefully and deliberately. In sending information and talking about the issue, use a credible voice (for example, think about the newscasters of the evening news programs). When talking with people, seeking information, and identifying solutions, use an approachable voice (for example, think about the hosts of the entertainment programs).

- *Use specific descriptions.* Specific language adds to the quality of communication because there is less left ambiguous. Clarity of intent and clarity of description are important facets to understanding issues. Being specific is key to clarifying issues and ensuring common understanding.

- *Position the body at 90 degrees.* This allows the speaker to point to the location of the visually displayed issue while pivoting and gesturing to the group. Ninety degrees is a natural placement for creating the third point. "Once the third point is created, then the rest of the components of How Not To Get Shot fall into place better" (Grinder, 1998, p. 33).

◈ Reflection

Think of a time when you had to deliver unwanted news or when you were in the audience receiving unwanted news. How was it delivered? Where was the messenger delivering the news? What nonverbal communication did he or she use in delivering the news? What happened in the group after the news was delivered?

Imagine a situation in the future when you may deliver a message that people really don't want to hear. How would you use each of the steps of HNTGS? What will you say, and how will you use your nonverbal communication to support your words? How might you expect the outcome to be different?

◈ Notes

_____

_____

_____

_____

_____

_____

_____

DAY 25
Handling Problems

Leadership has a harder job to do than just choose sides. It must bring sides together.

—Jesse Jackson

It is inevitable. Some groups will experience problems, such as breakdowns in communication, members who do not perform adequately, and misunderstandings about the work they are responsible for completing. It will be your responsibility to give them some help. What will you do? Here are some options:

• *If possible, anticipate and prevent the problem in the first place.* Although it is not always possible, many problems can be averted if a group has been formed properly and takes time up front to prepare to function as a team. For example, a group should make sure that it has the right mix of people, is clear about its purpose, and has sufficient resources. Members should take time to get to know each other and establish a set of norms for group behavior. If a group that you are responsible for hasn't taken these first steps, you are likely to encounter problems sooner or later.

• *Let the group deal with the problem.* Think of any problem as belonging to the group rather than to individuals. When a group has difficulties functioning, the source usually lies within the system rather than with individual group members. The group as a whole is often doing something that has let the problem develop or has exacerbated the problem. Therefore, it should be the group's responsibility to resolve it. If at all possible, help the members solve it for themselves.

• *Intervene if you think it necessary to get the group back on task.* Sometimes, the group can't solve the problem itself, and you will need to intervene. That intervention may be minimal or more extensive, depending on the nature of the problem.

• *Talk to some group members privately.* Either give them feedback about their own behavior or suggestions as to what they can do in the group.

• *Meet with the group.* You might simply observe the way a group functions and provide feedback. Or you may need to play a more assertive or confrontational role to help the group deal with its problem.

• *As a strategy of last resort, restructure the team by removing some people and/or adding others.* This approach, unfortunately, can tarnish a team's image and inhibit its functioning even though the team member or members are gone. (Scholtes et al., 1999, pp. 7.7–7.10)

◈ Reflection

Think for a moment of a group you were responsible for that had a problem. Was it a problem that could have been prevented? Did the group solve the problem itself? Did you have to intervene? What was the end result? What would you do differently the next time one of your groups encounters a problem?

◈ Notes

_____

_____

_____

_____

_____

_____

_____

_____

DAY 26

Dealing With Conflict

Conflict can be seen as a gift of energy, in which neither side loses and a new dance is created.

—Thomas Crum

Learn to love conflict! Yeah, sure. You must be kidding. Why should I learn to love conflict? Conflict is nothing but trouble.

Many of us have been conditioned to avoid conflict or become skillful in minimizing its impact. But there is a cost in doing so. Conflict that is suppressed or avoided tends to reappear. It often takes the form of passive-aggressive behavior in which a person appears to go along with a decision but then sabotages it. Avoiding conflict also lessens the chances that all alternatives will be explored and the most effective decision made.

Here are several common ways in which groups deal with conflict. All except one (possibly two) fail to resolve the issue:

• *Avoid the conflict.* Some people believe there is no value in attempting to bring conflict out in the open and resolve it. They may also be fearful of the consequences; therefore, they will attempt to avoid the conflict.

• *Smooth it over.* If the conflict can't be avoided, the next best strategy, according to the conflict avoiders, is to minimize the conflict so that relationships remain intact. There is an attempt to assuage individuals and move on. The real issues are never dealt with and are likely to resurface.

• *Force the conflict.* This strategy attempts to overpower group members to get them to accept a certain position. Personal relationships are disregarded; achieving the goal is more important. This is a competitive, win/lose approach that may backfire when the conflict reemerges.

• *Compromise.* In a compromise, the different sides each give up something for the greater good. Compromising is tricky. Sometimes it works; sometimes it doesn't. It can be either a lose/lose or a win/win strategy, depending on how much the different sides have to give up.

• *Problem solve.* Face the conflict head on and work through it. This strategy is the one that retains both personal goals and group relationships. It is most likely to produce a win/win outcome for all concerned. It does, however, require skill to be successful. Problem solving draws heavily on the norms of how people in groups talk to one another. (Scholtes et al., 1999, pp. 7.4–7.5)

Your approach to group conflict is a choice you make.

◈ Reflection

Think of situations in which groups you have been part of have encountered conflict. Which of the above approaches did your group take? With what results?

Which of the approaches listed is the one you naturally gravitate to? As a leader, one of your greatest gifts to your groups is your ability to face conflict directly and work through it. If you are not comfortable using problem solving in a conflict situation, what can you do to strengthen your confidence and comfort level and encourage the same in your group members?

◈ Notes

_____

_____

_____

_____

_____

_____

_____

DAY 27
Conflict as Opportunity

The question is not how to eliminate conflict but how to capitalize on its constructive aspects.

—Marion E. Haynes

A prerequisite to facing conflict directly and working through it is having a mindset of conflict as an opportunity. Conflict is a chance to look at situations from a new perspective and perhaps generate an entirely new solution. That is what conflict can provide, especially when people demystify conflict.

According to Garmston and Wellman (1999), conflict is nothing more than energy moving through a system. The meaning that people bring to the energy produces the conflict. And that meaning comes from one's own background, along with the culture of the group. Just as group members perceive reality through their own lenses, they also see conflict in highly individualized ways.

A useful distinction can be made between affective conflict and cognitive conflict. *Affective conflict* is interpersonal conflict. It is Harry and Jane versus Ralph and Denita, or the primary versus the intermediate team. This type of conflict deters group functioning. It contributes to decreased commitment, less cohesiveness, decreased empathy, and decisions that do not produce the desired results.

Cognitive conflict is a disagreement over ideas and approaches. It is a difference of opinion about, for example, how teachers should handle students' misconceptions in a constructivist approach to teaching and learning. This type of conflict is characteristic of a high-performance group. It separates the ideas from the people and holds the ideas up for close examination. It leads to greater commitment, increased cohesiveness, heightened empathy, deeper understanding, and decisions that produce the desired results.

Thus, one significant goal of an effective group is to increase cognitive conflict and reduce affective conflict.

▨ Reflection

Think about a group you have led that experienced some conflict. Was the conflict more affective or cognitive? How do you know? What happened? How was the conflict resolved—or was it?

How can you help a group avoid affective conflict and stay within the realm of cognitive conflict?

◈ Notes

_____

_____

_____

_____

_____

_____

_____

_____

_____

_____

DAY 28
Resolving Conflict

The doors we open and close each day decide the lives we lead.

—Flora Whittemore

As a leader, you have a responsibility to model conflict resolution directly. However, although you may be skillful in doing so, you may be dealing with other people who are not as skilled.

If emotions rise to the surface and interaction becomes heated, keeping yourself under control is a basic survival skill. It takes a high level of emotional maturity and some highly developed skills not to get sucked into the maelstrom of conflict. Here are some suggestions for remaining under control (Garmston & Wellman, 1999; Scholtes et al., 1999):

• *Breathe deeply.* Take a deep breath or two or three before saying a word. Under stress, our breathing becomes shallow, and oxygen is not distributed as well throughout our bodies.

• *Remember that the behavior of others is rarely malicious or evil in intent.* Most people are motivated by positive intentions.

• *Feel the energy of the conflict and move toward it rather than away.* Often in the midst of conflict, we want to retreat, to physically leave the premises, or at least to put some psychological distance between ourselves and the conflict. We are in a better position to dispel the conflict by moving toward and embracing it—physically and psychologically.

• *Know that the behavior of the people involved in the conflict is rarely planned, thought out, or calculated.* In most instances, conflict arises out of events, not deliberation.

• *Remember that conflict may stem from events, but it is not born out of the moment.* All conflicts have some history (for example, a previous conflict or negative experience).

• *Use paraphrasing.* Remember that paraphrasing shows the other person that you value his or her thoughts, feelings, and positions. It also helps you keep the focus off yourself and on the other person.

• *Try to keep the conflict cognitive in nature rather than affective.* Separate the issues from the people who are connected to them.

• *If you feel yourself "losing it," take a time out, at least for yourself and perhaps for the entire group.* Get a drink of water, make a trip to the restroom, or go outside for some fresh air.

◈ Reflection

In reviewing this list of suggestions, which ones do you use and feel comfortable with? Which ones might you try?

As a leader of groups, how can you help other group members use these techniques for themselves?

◈ Notes

_____

_____

_____

_____

_____

_____

_____

_____

DAY 29

Dealing With Disruptive People

Unprofessional behaviors noted during professional development sessions: Brings a laptop computer, not to take notes, but to play solitaire or other computer games; brings a pillow to the session, not to provide a softer seat, but as a headrest; and brings a Game Boy and plays continuously, occasionally cheering for himself.

—Thomas Guskey

As long as there are groups, there will be people in them who exhibit difficult behavior. Often, these individuals don't want to be in the group in the first place.

As a leader, you cannot allow the inappropriate behavior of a few people to control the group. There are constructive techniques for dealing with a person who is disruptive because he or she doesn't want to be part of the group:

• If people don't want to be in your group, confirm their sentiments rather than trying to convince them of the advantages of their participation. There may be individuals who prefer to be some place other than in your group, especially when participation is required. The best way to diffuse these people is to simply accept their feelings: "You're saying that you don't want to be here and that attendance creates a hardship for you. I'm not in a position, however, to do anything about that. Perhaps you should speak with . . ." Another possible response might go something like, "Yes, I know you resent the compulsory attendance policy. I hope you'll find something today that will be useful. If you have any specific questions or concerns, please see me at break." People will often drop their hostility once they have expressed their negative feelings, especially if you respond with a paraphrase.

• Deal directly with the person privately. If you chose the one-on-one approach, take the person aside. Try to determine the source of the person's behavior. Does he or she not want to be part of the group? If not, why not? Is it best for this person to leave? If he or she stays, what can mitigate the inappropriate group behavior? Does this person need anything from you or the group? If so, can you and/or the group provide the necessary support?

• Instead of dealing directly with a recalcitrant person, allow group pressure to emerge. Sometimes, approaching people directly is not the best strategy. Having group members deal with difficult individuals as peers may be much more effective. Members will often do this on their own; you need not do anything. If not, at some point you may want to turn to the group to ask members how they feel about something the difficult person has said or done. If the situation is best handled privately, you may want to ask one or two group members to speak to the person at the first opportune moment.

• Set up circumstances that allow people who should not be there to exit gracefully. If participation in the group is voluntary, a person may realize that he or she doesn't belong and leave. This can occur naturally when the group is establishing itself: clarifying purpose, adopting norms of behavior, assigning roles, and outlining tasks to be completed. An individual may see that participation just isn't appropriate or possible and withdraw from the group.

• Whatever strategy you choose for people who don't want to be there, use it promptly. By doing so, you establish the group as a safe place to work. Your actions show that you will not allow one or two people to disrupt the group's progress.

◈ Reflection

Consider this situation: You are co-instructor of a 6-week professional development series for elementary and middle school teachers. The focus is on incorporating algebraic concepts in grades K–7. The goal is to better prepare students for taking algebra in grade 8, which is now a required class unless students are specifically exempted.

There are 30 teachers signed up for the program, two from each elementary and middle school in your district. Most teachers volunteered to participate in the series; a few were appointed by their principals.

At the first meeting, you notice two people who act as if they don't want to be there. They fidget in their seats, read the newspaper, and occasionally just get up and leave for a short period. One is an elementary teacher; the other, a middle school teacher. You learn during the introductions that each was appointed by her principal to attend. During their introductions, you attempt to humor them, but they don't laugh.

As the day progresses, they continue their behavior. What do you do? What might you have done at the first indications of these individuals' unease?

◈ Notes

DAY 30

Presentation Skills

The key to successful leadership today is influence, not authority.

—Kenneth Blanchard

As a group leader (facilitator, presenter, coach, or consultant), your ability to influence others lies in how you present and conduct yourself, what you say, and what position you hold in the group and in your organization. Your most powerful source of influence is always how you present and conduct yourself; your behavior always speaks louder than your words. And your words have more ability to influence than your position of authority.

How long does it take to size up new group leaders? Probably just a few seconds after they speak a few words. Or judgment can be made simply by observing them for a few minutes before the meeting starts. On the basis of this initial impression, many group participants develop an opinion (positive or negative) about a leader. This opinion may change over time, but if it is negative, the leader must work harder to turn the image around.

What can you do in a session to help strengthen your image in a group? Here are some suggestions:

• *Greet and call group members by name.* To be recognized and called by name is a basic human need. Show your understanding of this by arriving at a meeting in time to greet people individually and call them by name. If you know them, you may also want to talk with each person briefly or make a comment that is relevant to each. If you don't know the people, introducing yourself before the meeting starts and learning members' names will strengthen your credibility. Following this suggestion will help you make a connection with the group and show that you value and respect each person.

• *Start with a strong opening.* Think about various meetings you have attended over the years, speeches people have made, or sermons you have heard—especially their beginnings. How many do you recall? How do most people start? Here are some examples of opening statements. Which do you see as strong? Weak? Why?

"Albert Einstein said, 'I never teach my pupils, I only attempt to provide the conditions in which they can learn.'"

"I really appreciate you giving up your Saturday morning to be with us."

"We want to start by introducing . . . and thanking the people who made today possible."

"I start by offering you a guarantee! By the time this session is over, you'll be able to . . . But if you can't, I'll refund . . ."

The ability to come up with a strong beginning is a real skill and one that anyone leading a group can develop with practice.

• *Get your participants speaking to each other or to you and the group as a whole after you make your opening comments.* The most powerful opening is one in which you make a few strong opening comments to establish both scope and tone for the meeting; then, get your participants talking. The earlier all voices are heard in the room, the better participation you will have. They may be talking with each other, perhaps introducing themselves or discussing their expectations for the meeting; or they may be speaking to the entire group and to you as the leader. Whatever the topic, they do the talking, not you.

This is very important because it establishes a participative tone for the meeting: It lets group members know that you are not going to stand in front of them and lecture the whole time. How many times have you heard group leaders say, "I'm not going to do all the talking, so I'll need to hear from each one of you"—and then talk at you for the next hour? By that time, you have taken in all you are able to and have lost faith in your facilitator. By involving the members, you are treating the group in a respectful manner. Moreover, you can gain their credibility by adhering to your word and making the session meaningful and relevant to them.

• *Eliminate tics from your speech or any annoying mannerisms.* Over the years, many people pick up "speech tics." These are superfluous words or sounds that work their way into our speech and become patterned responses. Can you spot the tics in the sentences below?

"Well, let me tell you about what happened in my organization."

"Let me tell—I want to tell—yes, I'll tell you about what happened."

"Uh, I want to tell you, uh, about what happened, uh, in my organization."

"You know, in my organization, the most wonderful thing happened. It was so unusual—you know—something that has never happened before."

We are often unaware of our tics, how often we use them, or how disruptive they are. Sometimes, listeners will be so distracted by the tic that they tune out the message. We may also have acquired some annoying mannerisms. Perhaps we look at one side of the room more than the other, use a pencil or pen in a distracting way, or stand in an awkward position. Just like the speech tics, these can detract from the positive impression we want to make on our group and more important, from the content of the presentation.

- *Conclude with a strong ending.* Think of various endings you have heard in speeches. Can you label the endings as either strong or weak? What made an ending strong? Here are some examples of concluding statements. Which do you see as strong? Weak? Why?

> "Thanks so much for coming. This was a good session. We'll meet again in two weeks. Don't forget to send me an e-mail if you have any questions."

> "I want to thank each of you today for your hard work. Roger, your intervention got us unstuck. Dale, Margaret, and Jennifer, each of you moved our work forward."

> "I want to close with a short poem I wrote last night about our charge."

> "Here are three cartoons that capture the essence of our work. Note in the first . . ."

◈ Reflection

Consider asking someone (ideally a colleague) to give you feedback on how you present yourself to a group. That includes your overall presence, how you meet and greet people, whether you have any tics in your speech or annoying mannerisms, and how you begin and end the meeting. If your colleague finds anything that needs improvement, monitor your own behavior closely. Then, ask for more feedback to see how you have improved.

◈ Notes

DAY 31

Six Domains of Group Development

When you start out in a team, you have to get the teamwork going and then you get something back.

—Michael Schumacher

So, once a group, always a group? Is this right?

Although the configuration may remain the same, group dynamics evolve. All groups attempt to balance getting the work done with attending to process, creating ongoing tension.

Six domains influence how effectively a group functions (Garmston & Wellman, 1999). For success in each domain, group members need to have domain-specific knowledge, skills, and structures. What follows is a brief explanation of each domain, its underlying assumptions, and what is necessary for the group to function effectively in that domain.

1. *Getting work done:* Group members understand that tension between task and process is ongoing and believe that it and the group's work are manageable. Key knowledge includes being able to function in modes of both dialogue and discussion, knowing how to conduct successful meetings, being able to facilitate groups, and skill in designing efficient and effective meetings.

2. *Doing the right work:* The underlying assumption here is that vision, mission, and values focus group energy and help ensure that they are doing the right work. Members need to know how to live with conflict, work with problems that seem unmanageable, increase their adaptivity, and create a sense of community.

3. *Working interdependently:* The key underlying assumption for this domain is that diversity is an asset and subgroups must work together and see each other as valuable resources. They must adhere to the seven norms of collaboration. They must also be proficient in discussion and dialogue, meeting management, facilitating groups, and living with conflict.

4. *Managing systems:* Knowing when to reject linearity and think more systemically and systematically as the tasks become more complex is the underlying assumption. Key knowledge includes living with conflict, handling unmanageable problems, being adaptive, and creating community.

5. *Developing groups:* Regardless of its current productivity, a group can always be more effective and/or more efficient. Adapting to change is a task for both individuals and groups. The underlying assumption is that both individual and group orientations are required to plan and implement significant change. The requisite knowledge includes information on these six domains, living with conflict, valuing community, and the principles for creating community.

6. *Adapting to change:* The underlying assumption here is that if groups are to be effective, they must constantly adapt to external environments. The more unstable the environment, the more the group must maintain an outward orientation. Required knowledge includes working with conflict, adapting to change, and creating community.

It is easy to see how interrelated these six domains are. For example, skill in dialogue and discussion are essential for two of the six. Being effective at dialogue requires internalization of the norms of collaboration. These are also prerequisites for dealing with conflict.

◈ Reflection

It is helpful to assess a group's stages of development in these six domains. Garmston and Wellman (1999) suggest a five-point rating scale set up on a continuum (see Table 4.1). Table 4.2 shows the ratings along the continuum, from "1: Beginning" to "5: Innovating."

Think of a group that you are part of. What do you see your group doing well? Where could your group function better? What knowledge and skills do you and your group members need that you don't have? What can you do to move your group forward?

Table 4.1   Assessing the Six Domains of Development

Domain	1	2	3	4	5
Getting work done					
Doing the right work					
Working interdependently					
Managing systems					
Developing your group					
Adapting to change					

SOURCE: Garmston, R. J., & Wellman, B. M. Copyright © 1999. *The Adaptive School: A Sourcebook for Developing Collaborative Groups* (p. 161). Norwood, MA: Christopher-Gordon. Reprinted with permission.

Table 4.2   Stages of Development

Stage of Development	Descriptor
1. Beginning	Unconscious incompetence (don't know what they don't know)
2. Emerging	Unconscious incompetence and conscious competence
3. Developing	Conscious competence
4. Integrating	Conscious competence and unconscious competence
5. Innovating	Unconscious competence

SOURCE: Garmston, R. J. & Wellman, B. M. Copyright © 1999. *The Adaptive School: A Sourcebook for Developing Collaborative Groups* (p. 161). Norwood, MA: Christopher-Gordon. Reprinted with permission.

▧ Notes

Bibliography

Argyris, C. (1986). Skill incompetence. *Harvard Business Review, 64*(5). (*Harvard Business Review* Reprint #86501)

Barth, R. S. (2003). *Lessons learned: Shaping relationships and the culture of the workplace.* Thousand Oaks, CA: Corwin.

Fullan, M. (2001). *Leading in a culture of change.* San Francisco: Jossey-Bass.

Garmston, R. J., & Wellman, B. M. (1999). *The adaptive school: A sourcebook for developing collaborative groups.* Norwood, MA: Christopher-Gordon.

Grinder, M. (1998). *Patterns of permission: The science of group dynamics.* Battleground, WA: Michael Grinder & Associates.

Mundry, S., Britton, E., Raizen, S., & Loucks-Horsley, S. (2000). *Professional meetings and conferences in education: Designing, planning, and evaluating.* Thousand Oaks, CA: Corwin.

Perkins, D. (1992). *Smart schools.* New York: Free Press.

Scholtes, P. R., Joiner, B. L., & Streibel, B. J. (1999). *The team handbook.* Madison, WI: Oriel.

Senge, P. M., Kleiner, A., Roberts, C., Ross, R. B., & Smith, B. J. (1994). *The fifth discipline fieldbook: Strategies and tools for building a learning organization.* New York: Doubleday.

Wheatley, M. J. (1992). *Leadership and the new science.* San Francisco: Berrett-Koehler.

Wheatley, M. (2002). *Turning to one another: Simple conversations to restore hope to the future.* San Francisco: Berrett-Koehler.

⬙ Index

**CORWIN
PRESS**

The Corwin Press logo—a raven striding across an open book—represents the union of courage and learning. Corwin Press is committed to improving education for all learners by publishing books and other professional development resources for those serving the field of PreK–12 education. By providing practical, hands-on materials, Corwin Press continues to carry out the promise of its motto: **"Helping Educators Do Their Work Better."**

NSDC's mission is to ensure success for all students by serving as the international network for those who improve schools and by advancing individual and organization development.